In the bestselling tradition of RUGBY SONGS, Warner presents a collection of vintage British humour collected from club rooms and pubs, from Land's End to John O'Groats.

Rugby Jokes

WARNER BOOKS

A *Warner* Book

First published in Great Britain by Sphere Books Ltd 1968
Reprinted 1969 (three times), 1970, 1971, 1973, 1976,
1978 (twice), 1979, 1980, 1981, 1983, 1985, 1986, 1987, 1988
Reprinted by Warner Books 1995

PUBLISHER'S NOTE
The Publishers acknowledge that some of the items in this volume may bear a
relationship, however denatured to other poems or stories actually written by people
intent on purposes other than conviviality. There may even be some of those authors
who, not being rugby fans, consider that the present version of their work deserves,
if not suppression, some acknowledgement to its original creator. In the absence of
such credit, which might in too many cases have justifiably annoyed the originator
from whose work the script here included was derived, the Publishers apologise to the
poets. If any of you who can prove ownership wish credit in the form of cash and
are prepared to come forward, at whatever risk to reputation or good name, the
Publishers are prepared to negotiate a reasonable settlement – quietly, and out of court

ISBN 0 7515 1548 5

Printed in England by Clays Ltd, St Ives plc
Set in Intertype Baskerville

RUGBY JOKES

"Rugby is a game played by men
with peculiarly shaped balls"

(William Webb Ellis)

RUGBY JOKES
AND COARSE LIMERICKS

Table of Contents

In Bed with the Doctor

A spinster suffered more and more from "nerves". She was not the doctor's best customer, so when the National Health came in he grew wearier than ever of her "nerves" and told her frankly that there was only one thing the matter with her.

"Doctor," she said, "I've left it too late, no face, no figure, who would take me to bed and perform, now?"

The doctor scratched his head.

"Doctor, would YOU do it, for twenty pounds?"

The Doc thought "Well, she's not as bad as all that, and it will work out at over a pound a minute" and said: "Yes, I'll call after surgery."

* * *

As she reached for her handbag to pay him, she said: "How about a repeat performance?"

"But Miss Rustyfan, you're a poor woman."

"Yes doctor, but I've saved up enough though to make sure of a respectable funeral; there' another twenty under the mattress, the Parish can bury me!"

BENDING OVER BACKWARDS

There was a sprightly old maid who lived to be a hundred, and all the Press men went after the story. One asked about her health. . . .

"I've never been to a doctor in my life!"

"Really Miss, in a hundred years do you mean to say that you were never bedridden, even for a short time?"

"Of course I was, young man, and table-ended, but there's no need to put that in the paper."

ILLUMINATING

A man went to his doctor, complaining of a pain in his member. The doctor examined him, and said:

"You can't be healthy without sex, what are you getting?"

The patient explained that he had a young lady, and went to the woods with her, twice a week.

"Yes, and does your member burn after intercourse?"

"I don't know doctor, I've never put a match to it."

INDEED I DO

There was an old specialist in the Diseases of Women, who simply could not stand the fat middle aged matron who ate and drank too much, and "never enjoyed good health". He could spot them a mile away.

One day he sat in his Consultant's chair at the hospital with students and nurses in attendance, when one such woman waddled up, and plonked her carcass in a chair without being asked. He went on writing, then suddenly looked up and said:

"Well, what's the matter with you!"

She sighed, rocked like a jelly, and said:

"Ooh doctor, you do feel terrible when you're on the change, don't you?"

"I do, I do, indeed I do!"

IT'S ALL MY EYE!

A hospital secretary moved to a new post, and decided immediately to tighten up on "security". He set up a man in the gatehouse with very strict instructions to challenge all comers. Those not on business were to be turned firmly away.

Quite soon a young woman marched up, seeking to enter.

"Hi, wait a bit, what's your business?" shouted the gatekeeper.

"I'm a maternity patient," said the girl.

"Can you prove it? are you pregnant?"

"Don't be daft, I haven't seen anything for six months."

"Ah, I thought so, you've come to the wrong place, the Eye Hospital's further down the road."

CONCRETE PROOF

A man went to the doctor and complained that he could not get an erection. The doctor gave him every treatment in the book, but none of them worked. After weeks of this, the doctor said:

"There's an old fashioned remedy which involves an injection in a very delicate place, but we'll try it."

It worked so well that the man had a permanent erection so that he asked for it to be reduced, if only for a time.

"Sorry my man, that's impossible."

"Surely doctor, to every known drug there is an antidote?"

"Yes, but this wasn't a drug."

"What did you inject it with then?"

"Just three of sand and one of cement."

YOU CAN KISS MY ARM

A man with a beautiful wife was in a car accident, and his wife's face was badly scarred. He went to the best plastic surgeon in the business to seek help.

"It will cost you three hundred pounds, but I can do it, if you will allow me to take the skin off your behind for grafting."

"Gladly!" said the husband, and so the operation was carried out, and it was a brilliant success; the wife was more lovely than ever.

The surgeon got a cheque for £400 and rang up to say:

"Hey, you sent me a hundred quid too much."

"Oh no I didn't, the extra hundred is for the sheer pleasure I get from watching my mother-in-law kiss my arse!"

RIDING FOR A FALL

The doctor told the working chap that he could not complete his examination without a sample of urine. The small boy who was sent with the "specimen" spilled most of it while messing about. Fearing a good hiding, he topped it up from a cow in a field.

The doctor hastily sent for the man, who returned home to his wife in a furious temper, and said: "That's you and your fancy positions! You would be on top wouldn't you, and now I'm going to have a baby."

STICKING OUT

A man was told by his doctor: "You are going to make medical history, you are the only male ever recorded who has become pregnant."

The man replied: "This is terrible, whatever will the neighbours say, I'm not even married."

SITTING IT OUT

An old lady went to the doctor because she was constipated.
"Well, d'you do anything about it?" he enquired.
  "Of course I do, doctor, I sit there for hours."
  "No, no, Mrs Bloggs, I mean, do you take anything?"
  "Oh yes, doctor, I takes me knitting."

ITHN'T IT NITH

The school doctor was examining a girl of goodly proportions, and, taking up his stethoscope, said:
  "Big breaths."
  "Yeth," said the girl, "and I'm not thixteen yet."

SHORT AND CURLY

There was a chap lay in hospital all too long, and he got very bored. One day out of devilment he said to a very straightlaced nurse: "Hey nurse, where does a woman's hair grow thickest and blackest and curliest?"
  The nurse coloured up, walked away, and came back with Matron. Said that dragon:
  "Young man, before I have you thrown out, tell me what you said, because nurse is too upset to repeat it."
  "Certainly Matron, I simply asked her where does a girl's hair grow thickest and blackest and curliest."
  "And where DOES it?" she said, outfacing him.
  "Why Matron, in Central Africa, of course!"

THE BALD TRUTH

An old Alderman found himself getting balder and balder. He couldn't bear the idea of taking his turn as Mayor, with a bald head, so he consulted his doctor. Said the quack:

"In the first place, nothing can be done, in the second place it's a sign of passion and you ought to be pleased."

The Alderman resigned from the Council, and spent the rest of his years and the rest of his fortune, searching for a bald woman.

A BLOODY MOUTHFUL

A woman went to the doctor and complained she could not get passionate. The doctor examined her, and told her that if she would follow his special diet she would get very randy. This was agreed, but after a few weeks she was back, and said:

"There's something gone wrong! Last night I got so passionate I chewed my boyfriend's ear off."

"Oh, don't worry about that trifle, it's only protein, no carbohydrates."

A BAREFACED LIE

Two Harley Street men were talking of professional difficulties. Said one who was a specialist in beauty treatment for rich women:

"You can't win, I warned Lady Mucke against having so many facelifts, but she would go on, and now she's suing me!"

"Really, what's the matter?"

"She's got a beard."

A LEAP IN THE DARK

A man came to the surgery covered with blood and bruises. . . . "What's the matter?" said the doctor.

"It's my wife – another of her nightmares!"

"Don't talk daft man! She might have kicked you, but not these injuries. . . ."

"Listen doc, she had one of her nightmares, she shouted out: 'Get out quick, my husband's coming home' and me being only half awake, naturally, I jumped straight out of the window."

FOR WHEEL OR FOR WOE

A man was off work without a medical note, and the foreman wanted an explanation . . .

"Where've you been, you lousy ignorant lazy B?"

"It was my wife Sir, she was giving birth to a wheel-barrow."

The foreman knew the man was stupid, but this was too much. . . . "If you can't do better than that, you'll get your cards, come on, what was the real trouble?"

The man pondered, and said: "I got it wrong, my wife was in bed having a pushchair."

"Go and get your cards! You're too dim even for this firm, you're fired!"

The labourer went home, and said: "Hes missus, what was wrong with you when you was poorly?"

"Jack, I told you, I had a miscarriage!"

"Ah, I knowed it was something with wheels on."

UNIDENTIFIED FLYING OBJECT

There was a young woman who did not seem very well, so her mother took her to the doctor. Mother did all the talking, she was that sort.

"She's pregnant," said the doc.

"Doctor, I must call you a fool, my daughter has never so much as kissed a man, have you darling?"

"No momma, I haven't even held a man's hand."

The doctor left his chair, walked to the window and gazed at the sky. There was a long silence, then mother asked —

"Is there anything wrong out there doctor?"

"Not at all, not at all! Only the last time this happened a star appeared in the east, and I don't want to miss it this time."

VIRGIN ON THE RIDICULOUS

An innocent young woman told her doctor she was not feeling at all well lately.

After examination, the doctor told her she was pregnant. . . .

"But that's impossible, I've never been with a man!"

The doctor patiently explained the facts of life to her in some detail.

"Well!" she said, "and that lousy First Aid Instructor told me it was artificial respiration."

ALL BALLS AND FESTIVITIES

A man went to the doctor with a pain in his loins.

After examination the doctor said: "You're a big man, doing a navvy's job, you need to wear a suspensory bandage."

"I'm on'y a hignorant navvy, wot's one o' them doctor?"

"Why man, it's a band for your balls, now good day, I'm busy."

The poor old navvy wandered around until by chance he came to a music shop, which was also an agency. There was a card in the window: BANDS FOR BALLS:

He went in, and said: "Is that right, bands for balls?"

"Yes indeed' said the bright and shapely girl behind the desk, "We have brass bands for large balls, and string bands for small balls, and . . .

"And," said the navvy, undoing his trouserflies, "what have you got for these?"

The modern miss did not bat an eyelid: "I'm afraid," she said, "You'll have to go to a sports shop and buy a hammock!"

STRETCHING IT A BIT

Said the plain nurse to the pretty nurse: "Hey, you know that big commando in the third bed?"

"Oh, you mean the one who's tattooed all over?"

"Yes, that's him, have you ever bathed him?"

"Yes, why?"

"Well, when I bathed him yesterday I noticed he had 'Ludo' tattooed on his er, thing."

"That's not 'Ludo', that's 'Llandudno'."

LIMERICKS I

There was a young man of Kings Lynn
Who was so exceedingly thin
That when he essayed
Making love to a maid
He slipped on the mat, and fell in!

There were two young ladies of Grimsby
Who wondered, what use could their quims be?
The bit in the middle
Was, clearly, for piddle,
But what could those hair-covered rims be?

There was a young curate named Batt
In the Lord Bishop's seat he was sat,
He was thinking of Venus
While pulling his penis,
And catching the drops in his hat

There was a young WAAF in the Ritz
Wearing officers' pips on her tits
A bit further down
Was an RSM's crown
Which gave further scope for the wits

There was young lady named Anna
Who thought she would like a pianner,
Her Mother said "No!"
And bought her a po
Saying "Now you can have a pee, Anna"

Pump! You Beggars Pump!

A certain tough old sea captain bought a young parrot at a foreign port (being assured it was a marvellous learner) and hung it on the bridge. Coming back through the Bay of Biscay, a fearful black cloud came over, and the skipper remarked: "It's gone bloody dark all at once." Soon after, the cloud burst in dreadful torrent, and the captain said to the mate: "It's bloody hissing down!" The storm got worse, the ship lurched and developed a leak, so that one of the men called up:

"What shall we do to be saved?" He got the reply: "Pump! you lousy shower! Pump you poxed-up beggars, pump!"

The ship, and all, were lost; a wet, swearing, washed-up parrot alone survived, and after some adventures, finished up with a dear spinster, who was just expecting the vicar. As a precaution she threw a cloth over the cage, so that the vicar was greeted with:

"It's gone bloody dark all at once."

The lady was livid, and put the parrot immediately under the cold water tap, at which he shrieked:

"It's bloody hissing down!"

"No, no, Miss Fantight! You mustn't be so cruel to God's creatures, rather bring him to church on the Sabbath, and expose him to good influences." This was done, and the parrot behaved like an angel, even joining in the hymns. The vicar, beaming at his own success, rose to announce his text: "Brethren today we ask What shall we do to be saved?" and down the aisles rang the parrot's clear tones. . . .

THE ARM OF THE LAW

There was a policeman with a dog on night duty, and he met up with a pretty young policewoman, also on night duty. It was a very cold night, and the policewoman was shivering. . . .

"What's the matter, can I do anything?"

The policewoman explained that she had come on duty late, and in a hurry, and had forgotten to put on her black woollen issue knickers. Being late already, she dare not go back and fetch them.

The dog handler said not to worry. He explained that the dog was superbly trained: "Let the dog sniff you between the legs, then we'll send him back to the station, and you can bet he'll return with your passion-killers."

This was agreed upon, and the dog trotted off, while they resumed their beat.

Half an hour later the dog returned, bearing part of the sergeant's hand!

SUCK IT AND SEE

A man went into his club leading a snake on a string.

The barman took a poor view of this, and fetched the Secretary, who said:

"Hey, is that snake poisonous?"

"Yes."

"Then what happens if he bites one of the members?"

"Oh that's no trouble, he just gets a friend to suck the wound."

"Suppose he gets bitten up the backside?"

"That's when he finds out who his friends are!"

IN DEATH AS IN LIFE

There was a spinster who kept a lady parrot and a gentleman parrot, which were her pride and joy. Then the lady parrot took cold and died, and, alas, the gentleman parrot died of a broken heart soon afterwards.

The spinster, very distressed, took the two dead birds to the taxidermist, so that they might be stuffed and preserved in the house as a memento.

"I'll send you a card in a week or so," said the man.

A month went by, with no news, so the spinster drove into town to enquire. "I forgot to ask you," said the taxidermist, "but do you want them mounted?"

"It's a nice thought," she said, "but the Vicar would never approve, so we'd better have them just holding hands."

TEARING A STRIP OFF

The costermonger had a donkey, and one day the animal said:

"Hey, it's twenty years today I've worked for you, in all weathers."

"So you have," said the cockney, "what can I get you for a special treat?" – "A night with a female," said the ass. So the cockney scoured London, but he could not find a female donkey on hire. When he had given up hope, he came to a circus, where the boss said that for £5 he'd loan out a female zebra.

The cockney took the zebra, shoved it in the stable, and went home for a late supper. Next day, he asked the moke: "How'd you get on – alright?"

"Bloody awful, I couldn't get her pyjamas off."

MEN SELDOM MAKE PASSES ... ?

The spinster had a parrot who kept repeating:

"I want to poke, I want to poke."

She found this slightly irritating, until a married friend explained what it meant, then she became very alarmed. . . .

"I love that bird, but I'll have to get rid of him, or the vicar will never call again," she said. But her more experienced friend said:

"Well, if you really love him, you'll get him what he longs for, which is a female, then he won't keep on about it all the time." Off went the spinster to the bird shop, but the man said: "No can do, no lady parrots coming in at all this season Miss, but I can do you a lady owl at a reasonable price."

Anything was better than nothing, so she popped the owl into the parrot's cage, and waited with thrilled anticipation. . . .

"I want to poke, I want to poke," said the parrot.

"Oooh, Ooh," said the lady owl.

"Not you, you goggle eyed freak," said the parrot, "I can't stand women who wear glasses."

A LOT OF BULL

A city visitor, a ventriloquist, was being shown round a farm. For a joke he made the bull appear to say: "How d'ye do". The attendant yokel did not seem impressed, until the hen said: "Hodge has been stealing my eggs," when he became very flustered, and the farmer said:

"Hodge, what have you to say to that, hey?"

"What I says to that master's this, when you gets to that young sow across the yard, don't you believe a word her tells ye, because it ain't true."

SERVED HER RIGHT!

The new young farmer was all for modernisation. The first thing he did was to put radio on in the cowsheds, and the effect of the music was greatly to increase milk output. He was so pleased that he went over to TV, and although the farm-hands scoffed, he scored once more, with a higher yield.

Then he achieved his greatest ambition, sold the bull, and went in for A.I.D. Much to his distress, milk output dropped to an all-time low.

One day a labourer rushed in and said: "Master, I don't know why 'tis, but they cows are giving double milk today, I've never know'd anything like it."

The farmer ran down to the cowsheds, and the first thing which caught his eyes was the TV, which was reading:

"Normal service will shortly be resumed."

HORSE SENSE

There was a Vicar who was always being approached by young people in his flock as to whether it was or was not better to have sexual experience before marriage.

As he knew little of these matters he wrote to an old college friend who was now a Consultant Psychologist, and he finished: "When you write back, phrase it tactfully, as my wife reads all my letters."

The Psychologist wrote back:

"Dear Revd. John,

There was once a recruit who joined the cavalry. The sergeant said: 'Have you ever ridden a horse before?' and the young man said 'No', so the sergeant said: 'Here's a horse that's never been ridden, you can start together'."

There was a man whose wife had a pet parrot, but it died, and she was very upset. Her good natured husband went off to the shop to get another bird, but nothing the man had on offer would do. One was too dear, one was too dull, another too big, until the Pet Shop man was fed up, and the customer made for the exit.

In the doorway he saw a parrot he really fancied:

"How much for this chap," he asked.

"That's a very special parrot; I don't really want to part with it, but if I do, it's £200."

"What's so very special about it?"

"Well, you see Sir, she's the only parrot in Great Britain that lays square eggs!"

The caller was not disposed to believe this, but the vendor took him into the back room, and showed him a dish of eggs, each a perfect cube.

"It's a deal, I'll take the bird with me," he said.

While the shopkeeper was making out the bill, an uneasy thought struck the man (thinking of his wife) and he said:

"I suppose the parrot can talk, as well?"

"Well, Sir, she can, but so far she only seems to have one expression."

"Oh indeed, what's that?"

"Ooooo Ooooo Ker – rist!"

NUTS TO YOU TOO

There was a workingclass Cockney who had given his young son a big build-up about the monkeys at the Zoo. If only the lad would be good, Dad would take him on Saturday to the Monkey House at Regents Park.

The kid was good, Saturday came, and off went the two of them to the Zoo. Alas! there was not a monkey in sight. This made Father very angry, and he fetched a Head Keeper. . . .

"Well, of course," said the Keeper, this happens to be the breeding season – they're all inside the hut."

"Do you think they'd come out for a nut?"

"Well, would you?"

SORRY FRED

A man had a buck rabbit at stud, and one day the buck complained of overwork. . . . "I want an assistant," he said.

"How could I get another as gentlemanly as yourself?"

"You buy a healthy young buck, I'll teach him good manners," said the rabbit, "if you pop him in with me."

This was done, and the man stood back to listen. . . . "Tomorrow there will be a row of does lined up; I'll start at one end, you at the other, and just remember your manners. "You will say, 'darling that was divine' or 'thanks a million' or something, but don't forget manners manners."

Next day early, the owner dropped the bucks, one at each end of the row of does, and was astonished to hear: "Ta duck, ta duck, ta duck, ta duck, SORRY FRED, ta duck, ta duck. . . ."

There was a young lady of York
Seducing herself with a cork,
It stuck in her vagina
And can you imagine 'er
Probing it out with a fork!

There was a young girl of Kinsale
Who offered her body for sale,
To be kind to the blind
She engraved her behind
With detailed instruction in Braille.

There was a young lady named Starkie
Who had a night out with a darkie
The result of her sins
Was quads and not twins,
One black, one white, and two khaki!

There was a young lady at sea
Who said: "It is so hard to pee"
"Oh indeed?" said the Mate,
"That accounts for the state
Of the Captain, the Purser, and me."

There was a young girl of Dumfries
Who said to her boyfriend "Oh, please,
It will give me great bliss
If you play more with THIS,
And give less attention to THESE."

Nicer than Pork, isn't it

A priest and a rabbi happened to find themselves sharing a first class carriage on a long rail journey. They argued without rancour about the truths of religion, until the priest, feeling he was getting the worst of it, said rather sharply:

"Look here rabbi, on your oath as a man of religion, can you swear you never enjoyed the taste of pork?"

The rabbi coloured up, wrestled with his conscience a moment, and said:

"Very well Father, I'll admit it, I have eaten pork."

"And it's very nice, isn't it!" exclaimed the triumphant man of Rome. The rabbi retired behind his Jewish Times in a long and thoughtful silence. Suddenly re-emerging he said:

"I say Father. . . ."

"Yes brother, what is it?"

"Can you swear as a Christian priest that you have never enjoyed sex with a girl out of the flock?"

The priest tried to beg off, but the rabbi insisted:

"The truth, come on, the truth?!"

"Well rabbi, I confess it, I have."

"Nicer than pork, isn't it?!"

MATERNAL CARE

The Curate reading the Church Notices: "Next Sunday is Easter, will those ladies who have eggs please lay them in the church porch: The Young Mothers meet each Wednesday, will those who wish to become young mothers, please meet me in the vestry any Tuesday evening."

A DELIGHTFUL SPOT

A curate went on his honeymoon to a Lakeland hotel. As he was a natural early riser, he came down before breakfast after his bridal night, and found the lounge deserted, except for a regular resident, an old retired Army Officer. The officer looked across at the vista of lakes and mountains in the clear air, and remarked:

"A delightful spot Sir!"

"Yes indeed," said the curate, "and so cunningly concealed."

THE WORM TURNED

A woman died and went up to the Pearly Gates. Saint Peter came out, and said: "Come in."

"I want you to find my husband," said the woman, "I can't be happy unless we are reunited."

"What was his name?" said the Gate Keeper.

"Why, Smith," she said.

"Upon my everlasting soul! we've millions of Smiths in Heaven. Had he any distinguishing peculiarity?"

"He was a most peculiar man, his last words were, 'Missus, if you're ever unfaithful, I shall turn in me grave."

Peter said: "Oh, you mean *revolving* Smith."

A GOOD MAN AT BOTTOM

The Vicar had been prominent in local affairs for many years, so when he retired a dinner was given in his honour, by the Council he had so ably chaired.

The Distinguished Guest was no Churchman, but he thought that in thanking the Vicar he must work in a religious reference. Unfortunately the wine had gone round too often, and he said:

"Ladies and gentlemen, when a child is born its Guardian Angel gives it a kiss; if it is kissed on the head it will be brainy, if on the mouth, a good singer, if on the hands a clever craftsman. I don't know where our Vicar was kissed, but he certainly makes a damn good Chairman!"

USUAL PERFORMANCE

An earnest spinster wanted to work on a newspaper. She had no experience, but as her father was a Bishop and very influential in the district, they took her on.

Her first assignment was to write up the wedding of a young actor and actress who were prominent in the local Repertory Company. Said the Editor:

"Your angle on this is: 'The Show Must Go On' – write it up from that point of view."

She wrote: "Sally Promptside married Arthur Script at Mugsborough Register Office this afternoon. The usual performance will take place tonight."

ALL BULL

A girl about eleven was walking down the village street leading a cow on a rope. She met the Vicar, who said: "Little girl, little girl, what are you doing with that cow?"

"Please sir," said the child, "it's my father's cow, and I'm taking it to the bull."

"Disgusting, disgusting," said the parson, "can't your father do it?"

"No indeed Vicar, it has to be the bull."

OLD AGE WENCHIONER

There was a very old parson who married an innocent girl of eighteen. He took her off on honeymoon, and soon had her to bed.

She said: "Ooh dear, I do feel something strange coming over me," and he said: "Yes, it's old age creeping on."

VICE – VERSA!

There was a girl married a curate and when he got her to bed he seemed to know his way around with a great deal of expertise. She said:

"Darling, have you ever done anything like this before?"

The question took him by surprise, and he coloured up.

The girl, pressing home her advantage said: "Come on, come on, own up, own up, we must start with a clean sheet, who WAS it?"

After a deal of stammering and stuttering he said it was with one of the choir boys.

Writing to her mother the next day, the bride said: "Do you know, I didn't know which way to turn."

COCKSURE

A young woman was alone in a railway carriage until a clergyman got in. Seeking to be sociable, he said:

"That's a fine baby you've got there."

The woman replied that it was indeed a lovely child, conceived after six years of marriage, when hope had almost gone.

"Yes," said the parson, "persistence, persistence, is always blessed in the end; take my case, I breed pigeons; for years I never won a race, but lately I'm winning silver cups all the time."

"Indeed," said the young married woman, "what made the break-through?"

"Oh, I changed the cock."

"Yes, that's what I did."

TIME FLIES

It was the Rugby Club dinner, and the main speaker, a Bishop, was drivelling on and on. . . . On the right of the chairman sat the Mayor.

"I wish to cripes I knew how to stop the beggar," said the first to the second. "That's easy," said the experienced old Mayor, "pass that paper serviette," upon which, he scribbled a few words and passed the note to the speaker.

The speaker, in full flow, glanced, suddenly mumbled a conclusion, and sat down. Said the chairman to his friend: "You're a genius, what did you write?"

"Only four little words – 'Your flies are undone.' "

SHE HAD GOOD PULL

The Mothers Union were on their annual coach outing, and unfortunately Mrs Bloggs began to tipple. Indeed, after the last stop, which was at a truly rural pub, they couldn't find Mrs Bloggs at all.

The Vicar said he would go and look for her, and, wandering round the back of the "Farmers Arms" he found a cowshed in which was a cow. Hanging onto the cow's teat was Mrs Bloggs.

"Come along now dear," he said, "come and get in your seat like a good woman."

"Shan't move," said Mrs Bloggs in a very slurred voice. "Shert'nly not. I sat by the driver coming along, I shall sit by the driver goin' back."

TENORS – AND BASS

The new doctor was making his first-ever round of the Maternity Ward. Seeking to be friendly, he asked the woman in the first bed when her baby was due.

"March 11th," she said. The next woman he came to said her event would be March 11th, and so it went on.

"Extraordinary!" said the doctor to the Matron, "extraordinary coincidence." However, the last patient he spoke to said her due date would be March 17th.

"That's more extraordinary still, that nineteen women should be on the same date and just the twentieth should be different."

"Ah well, you see doctor, I wasn't on the Choir Outing."

HE WAS A BAR – STEWARD

There was a man went to his Club on a weekday to play golf, and the only person available was a parson, a stranger who had called in while on holiday.

Off they went, and the man said: "Ah, reverend, I hope you don't mind, but we always play for a pound in this club."

The parson was put out, not approving of gambling, but he thought "only a pound", and teed up. His opponent played dirty, sneezed at the wrong moment, used filthy language, cheated when he could, and finished up thrashing the poor old parson. . . ."In this Club, the loser buys the drinks" he told him, adding: "And may I trouble you for six quid."

"I thought we agreed a pound?"

"A hole!" said the villain.

Over the drinks, the cad said: "If you're ever this way again vicar, drop in and I'll always gladly give you a game."

"Yes," was the reply, and here's my card, come to my church, and it would be a good idea if you brought your parents, too."

"Brought my father and mother? Why?"

"Well, I could marry them."

SOME'S SPEED!

The Mothers' Meeting were on their annual coach outing, and unfortunately the driver was a reckless sort, and drove faster and faster.

Down one narrow winding lane in Wales he was getting up to sixty mp.h. when the Dear Vicar observed that old Mrs Moggs had gone white in the face with fear. He went up, put his arm on her shoulders and said, with a great show of jocularity: "Some speed, eh Mrs Moggs, some speed!"

"I don't know about the others, Vicar, but I certainly have."

A HARD PROPOSITION

A parson was anxious that the church social and dance should be a success. An actress famous for her voluptuous figure was doing a local show, and he got her to support it. The lady was wearing a tight sheath dress with a daring corsage, and as she and the vicar led off in the first dance he remarked:

"You know, Miss Tartly, you're a wonderful actress."

"Thank you vicar."

"And you are also very beautiful."

"That's nice of you vicar," and they danced on. "But I ought to tell you," he went on, blushing, "that I've got just one thing against you."

She said: "Yes, I can feel it."

A MAN OF POSITION

This same vicar thought he ought to do something to "save" this actress, and he innocently suggested to her that he should visit her in her room, to "get down to fundamentals".

She readily agreed, and when the vicar arrived she was stark naked on the bed with her legs wide open.

"I prayed for you all last night . . ." he began.

"Well, I'm on the phone, but anyway, you can have me now for five pounds."

"No no Miss Tartly, you misunderstand, I expected to find you on your knees, and I think that even now we should begin by kneeling down."

"Of course vicar, if that's how you want it, but it hurts a bit, and anyway if you want it kinky it's ten pounds."

JIMMY'S RIDDLE

A curate went to his first parish, and was met by the vicar, who said: "Ah James, you've just come at the right moment, the Parish Mothers are having their weekly meeting in the Hall, you must go down and introduce yourself to them."

When the curate entered the Parish Mothers' meeting the cackle suddenly stopped, and there was an embarrassed silence. The curate beamed round the room, and said:

"Well well, I can see we're all knitting or sewing, but can't someone tell a story or ask a riddle to enliven the proceedings?"

"Yes," said old Mrs Bloggs in the corner, "you've been to college, what is it a man stands up to do, a woman sits down to do, and a dog holds out his leg to do?"

Scarlet and stammering, the curate blurted out that he had not the least idea. . . .

"Why!" said the old gossip, "to shake hands, of course!"

COMING WITH A LETTER

The wealthy widow of a Rural Dean was explaining her duties to the new housemaid. The widow would be lying in bed late each morning, the maid would bring her up a cup of tea, and should then go back down and fetch the post, for she was a massive correspondent.

The girl listened carefully, and followed her instructions, except that she didn't come back up again:

"Mary, Mary! Hasn't the postman come yet?"

"Not yet Mum, but he's breathing hard."

TAKING THE MICKY

There was a young nun who went to the Mother Superior in some distress, and after a great deal of beating about the bush, admitted she was pregnant.

"Who was it? Who was this wicked wicked man?" said the Mother Superior.

"Oh Reverent Mother, I wouldn't commit a carnal offence with a man!" exclaimed the nun.

"Well it wasn't fathered by a woman, was it!" said the M.S., beginning to lose her temper.

"No indeed blessed mother, but it was fathered by one of the Holy Angels" (simper, simper).

"Holy Angels – what is this nonsense?"

"Yes Blessed Mother, he came down to me in the middle of the night in my sleep, and when I asked him who he was he said "Saint Michael" and showed me his name on his vest, to prove it."

WHITE FRIARS

There was a man went to a laundry for a job, and the Manager said: "Trade's terribly slack, but if you can fetch in any fresh business, I'll give you 5% on the take."

"That's me!" said the man, "the best order-getter in the business," and off he set, whistling. He was back in half an hour with a black eye.

"Hallo," said the Manager, "what's going on?"

"Well Sir, I thought I'd try that monastery down the road. I asked to see the Father Superior, and when I was admitted I said I felt sure the monks must have some dirty habits."

PUNCTURED

The parson was a worried man, "Listen," he said to his verger, "somebody's stolen my bicycle."

"Where've you been on it rector," enquired that worthy.

"Only round the parish on my calls."

The verger suggested that the best plan would be for the rector to direct his Sunday sermon to the ten commandments. . . . "When you get to 'Thou Shalt Not Steal', you and I'll watch their faces, we'll soon see."

Sunday came, the rector started in fine flow about the Commandments, then lost his thread, changed the subject, and tailed off lamely.

"Sir," said the verger, "I thought you was going to. . . ."

"I know Giles, I know, but you see, when I got to 'Thou Shalt Not Commit Adultery' I suddenly remembered where I'd left my bicycle."

FISHY STORY

The Trappists needed something for supper, and the Father Abbot made signs to two of the monks to go out early and fish.

They fished silently all day without a single bite, and were thoroughly fed up, when, at the end of the day, the younger monk caught a mermaid. He looked at this naked and beautiful catch, fondled it all over, then hurled it back into the lake.

The other Trappist could keep his fearful vow of silence no longer, he exploded:

"Why?"

"How?"

THE BEST OF THE RUBBER

To a highly select parish in Cheltenham came a new curate who, within a short time married a sexy young woman. In ten months they had a child, and eleven months after that, another. At the end of five years they had five children and were expecting a sixth. The worthies of the parish were deeply shocked, and wrote to the Bishop about it.

The Bishop sent the curate a strong letter.

HE WAS STONED

When the new curate arrived, the vicar said:

"I'm giving you a break, the Bishop's coming next Sunday, I'll stand down for you; this will be your great chance to get marked for preferment."

By Sunday the curate was a nervous wreck, but the vicar he'd been through it all and knew the answer, with which he took the curate into the vestry.

"As you preach and your mouth goes dry, take a sip of this", and he gave him a glass of water well laced with gin. But his hand slipped and he overdid the gin.

The curate preached like a fireball, then, lurching down, staggered to the Bishop, slapped his back and said: "Not a bad shermon, eh m'Lord, hey? hic!"

"Ah, a fair start my son, but you know, there were ten commandments not twelve, twelve apostles not ten, and David slew Goliath with a stone, he did *not* do up the stupid bleeder with the jawbone of a bloody ass."

THE LONG AND THE SHORT OF IT

A young hardworking and devout farmer in the Irish village shocked the priest by marrying a girl from away, and a Protestant at that. However, much to his relief, the girl became a Catholic.

In his middle age the farmer lost his wife; again he married a stranger and a Protestant and shocked the priest, but she too was converted.

In his old age the same thing happened, but the priest did not worry, until several months passed, and the new bride did not come to mass. He then went and gave Patrick a piece of his mind . . .

"Jabers father, the old converter isn't what it was!"

THE SEX MANIAC

The newly appointed priest thought he'd walk this vast parish and meet the flock. One day he followed a dusty track for miles to find a devout family with fourteen children.

"Good day Connelly, you're a credit to Ireland, the biggest family in the parish."

"Good day father, but this is not the biggest family in the parish – that's Doylan, over the hill."

It was a tired priest who greeted Doylan and his sixteen children, but . . . "God bless all these eighteen little Catholics" he said.

"Sorry father, but this is a Protestant family!"

"Then I'll go at once," said the priest, "for it's nothing but a dirty sex maniac that ye are!"

CIRCUMSCRIBED

A rabbi and a priest were neighbours, and there was a certain amount of "needle" between them. If the Cohens had their drive done up, Father O'Flynn had his relaid, and so it went on.

One day the priest had a new Jaguar, so the rabbi bought a Bentley. When the rabbi looked out of his window it was to see the priest pouring water over the top of the car bonnet. He opened the window and shouted:

"That's not the way to fill the radiator, you know."

"Aha," said the priest, I'm christening it with holy water, that's more than you can do to yours."

A little while later the priest was taken aback to see the rabbi lying in the road, hacksaw in hand, sawing the last inch of his car's exhaust pipe.

THE LITTLE MOTHER

A sincere clergyman was out walking when he saw three Salvation Army girls sitting on a bench crying their eyes out. He lifted his hat, saying: "Pardon me, but this is a wretched sight, can I help?"

There was no reply, only more sobs.

He tried again: "Over there in the pavillion we can have a nice cup of tea, that always improves things."

When the tea and cream cakes arrived the girls cheered up. As the waitress put the tray down, the parson beamed and said:

"Who's going to be the 'little mother'?"

They all burst into tears again.

A FOUR-LETTER WORD!

A curate and a bishop were in opposite corners of a railway carriage on a long journey. As the bishop entered, the curate put away his copy of "Playboy" and was reading the "Church Times". The bishop ignored him, and went on doing the "Times" crossword. Silence prevailed.

After a while the curate tried to make conversation, and when the bishop began to do a lot of head scratching and "tut-tut-tut-ing" he tried again. . . .

"Can I help you Sir?"

"Perhaps; I'm only beaten by one word; what is it that has four letters, the last three are U, N, T, and the clue is: 'Essentially feminine'?"

"Why Sir," said the curate after a slight pause: "that'll be 'Aunt'."

"Of course, of course!" said the bishop, "I say young man, can you lend me a rubber?"

T-T-T-T-TEE TOTALLER!

A shy young curate went to a strange golf club while on holiday, and asked the Secretary to find him a game. The Sec. was very busy, and said:

"Look here, there's a pretty girl just gone out, she's a stranger like you, catch her up and introduce yourself."

So the shy young man went after the girl and said:

"M-my name's P-peter, b-but I'm n-no s-saint."

The girl replied with a flashing smile:

"M-my name's M-mary, b-but I'm n-not a v-v-v-very g-good player!"

SHOTGUN WEDDING?

A pretty young married woman went to her vicar and asked for some advice. She did not wish to start a family yet, and (putting the matter delicately) asked the parson if he knew how to prevent the stork from settling on the roof.

The vicar said that as an old bachelor he could not answer the question, but his sister had a very wise parrot, Oxford educated, and they had best ask the bird.

The parrot, duly put in humour by sugar, cocked his head when the vicar said:

"Polly, tell the young lady how to prevent the stork from landing" and shouted:

"Shoot it in the air!"

CONVENT-IONAL

The nuns ran an orphanage, and one day the Mother Superior summoned to her office three buxom girls who were leaving, and said:

"Now, you're all going out into the big sinful world, and I must warn you against certain men. There are men who will buy you drinks, take you to a room, undress you, and do unspeakable things to you. Then they give you two or three pounds, and you're sent away, ruined!"

"Excuse me Reverend Mother," said the boldest one, "did you say these wicked men do this to us and give us three pounds?"

"Yes, dear child, why do you ask?"

"Well, the priests only give us apples."

LIMERICKS III

There were two young ladies of Birmingham
There is a good story concerning 'em,
They lifted the frock
And played with the cock
Of the Bishop engaged in confirming 'em;
Now, the worthy old Bish was no fool
(He'd been to a Sec. Modern school)
He took off the britches
Of those dirty bitches
And used his episcopal tool!

There once was a wicked old actor
Who waylaid a young girl and attacked 'er,
In reply to this trick,
She bit off his wick
And thus remained virgo intacta!

There was a young man of Cape Horn
Who wished he had never been born,
He wouldn't have been
If his father had seen
That the end of the letter was torn

There was a young plumber named Lee
Who was plumbing his girl by the sea,
When she said: "Stop your plumbing!
"There's somebody coming!"
Said the plumber (still plumbing) "It's me!"

Nuts Screws Washers and Bolts

A certain rich man had a wastrel son who was the family's despair. Finally, the old man, whose name was Nuts, bought his son a laundry business in a remote country town, also appointing a reliable manager. All was peace for a time; then came an urgent call from the manager to go down at once. Sure enough, the manager was at the station:

"It's terrible Sir, your son has put half the laundry girls in the family way."

"That's bad, but could be worse."

"Worse than that Sir, he's scarpered, gone away!"

"That's bad, is that the lot?"

"Much worse Sir, the local paper's on to the story, and they're going to splash it. . . ."

The old man was sure there was nothing money could not do, so he called on the local editor, and offered a good bribe to suppress the scandal, "for the sake, not of my worthless son, but his ailing mother."

The editor said too much was known already, he dare not kill the story, but for a hundred quid he could print it in a form well understood in the town, but not likely to be picked up by the National press.

This being agreed, an anxious father awaited the week-end and read: "Special Ironmongery Announcement – NUTS SCREWS WASHERS AND BOLTS".

GOOD FOR NOTHING

In a first-class carriage rode an icy Deb, very "top drawer". Opposite was a middle aged business man. Suddenly he lowered his Financial Times and said:

"Would you sleep with me just one night for a thousand pounds?"

The snooty girl said any more of this talk and she would pull the alarm cord! The man smiled patiently and said: "Money is nothing to me if I fancy anything, and I fancy you . . . TEN thousand pounds?"

The girl was beginning to waver, and he pressed:

"At the Hilton, in pound notes, cash in advance?"

After a little more hesitation the young lady said yes, the deal was on.

"Right, will you get down on the seat now, for thirty bob?"

"My dear Sir, how dare you! What sort of person do you think I am?!" she blazed.

"Now now, that's already settled, we're merely haggling on price."

GONE TO POT

A man narrowly reared by a widowed mother, got married. He telephoned back to his mother from the honeymoon hotel, to say that he knew there was something he had to do in bed, but he didn't know what it was.

"Why," said his mother, "you put your . . . er, that is, you put the hardest part of yourself in the place where your wife wee-wees."

At midnight the hotel rang the Fire Brigade for help. . . .

"We've got a young man with his head jammed in a chamber-pot."

FAST AND LOOSE

A noble lord whose wife had died, was making all arrangements for his daughter's "coming out". At the last moment he was sent for on urgent government work, so he asked the butler – a faithful old family retainer – to see that the Coming Out Ball details were finalised and keep an eye on the daughter.

The Deb daughter went to her Ball, and she did not come back until 3 a.m. When she awoke, very late, she was in bed, and the faithful retainer was standing by with black coffee. . . .

"James, how did I come to be in this bed?"

"You came home very late and very tired, my lady."

"But James, I'm undressed and in my nightdress!"

"I could not let you spoil that dress, my lady."

"Good lord James, do you mean you undressed me and put me to bed without my knowing it?"

"Yes Madam."

"James, tell the truth, was I tight?"

"Not after the first time, my lady."

IT'S A WISE CHILD

A certain little girl, when asked her name, would reply:

"I'm Mr Smithbrown's daughter."

Her mother told her this was wrong, she must say:

"I'm Jane Smithbrown."

Then the Vicar spoke to her in Sunday School, and said: "Aren't you Mr Smithbrown's daughter?"

She replied:

"I thought I was, but mother says I'm not."

THE STUPID COUNT

A sweep's son was his mother's only darling, and when they won the pools, mother insisted the boy must go to college, although father protested.

The son sent home for rowing togs, cricket togs, tennis togs, and no matter what father said, Willy was refused nothing. Finally, he wrote and said the college ball was coming due, could he have a suit of tails. Father went mad, but mother sent the money.

The boy wrote to say that he had been a great success at the Ball. . . . "Everybody said I looked like a proper Count," he wrote.

"He never could spell," said his father.

WIRE PULLING

A pompous self-made grocer named Bates got his son into a posh college. Of course, the whole family had to go up with Johnny, to see him start his first term, and to meet the Principal.

"I'm Sir Snortweight Bates," announced the rich grocer, "this is my good lady, Lady Bates, my daughter, Miss Bates, and my son Master Bates."

"Oh does he? Well, we'll soon get him out of that."

IN PRAISE OF VICE

It was a Tory convention, and the President introduced a smashing matron, "and I must tell you that Lady Goodbody is also chairman of the Northern Federation."

"No no," said the speaker, "Sir Bragge Bloodworthy is our chairman, I am his vice. . . ."

TOWN AND GOWN

The Oxford student was walking out late at night with a sleazy blonde on his arm, when he ran straight into the proctor: "Sir!" said the proctor, "are you a member of this University?"

"Yes, Sir, I am."

"Then introduce me to the young gentlewoman."

(The undergrad was a quick thinker . . .). "Certainly Sir," he said, "this is my elder sister. . . ."

"Gosh dammit," said the proctor, beginning to lose his temper, "everybody knows this is the most notorious old bag in Oxford!"

"Oh Sir, how unkind of you to throw the family misfortunes into my face in such a manner."

PROCTOR-COL

The proctor was prowling along the river bank at night, seeking whom he could catch, and he came to a punt tied up in some bushes. He could just make out a scholastic gown and a pair of silken legs.

The proctor turned to his bulldogs (strong-arm men) and said: "Fetch him here!" The unfortunate fellow was lifted off and placed in a dishevelled state before the proctor. In accordance with ancient protocol he asked the time-honoured question: "Sir, are you a member of this University?"

"Gore dammiy and suck yourself!" stormed the angry victim, "I am chairman of the governing body of this university!"

The proctor turned calmly to the bulldogs and said:

"Replace the gentleman."

"EXCEEDINGLY SMALL. . . ."

The Proctors of Cambridge were watching a house of ill repute to see if they could catch any undergrads using it. They hid in a doorway and saw three young men enter; after an hour one came out. . . .

"Your name and college sir ?"

"Smith of Jesus," he said.

Two hours went by before the second victim came out, and it was getting dark and cold when he admitted to being "Jones of Trinity."

It was two in the morning, and snowing before the last one was caught: "You needn't tell us," they said, "you're Mills of God."

!VE LA DIFFERENCE!

A stodgy professor, in Paris on business, was approached at night by a girl offering her charms for cash. The prof stuttered:

"I don't understand you, and I've left my dictionary at the hotel." The girl lifted her skirt and said: "Voici le dictionaire universel, qui les savants de tout pays ont ouvert" (Behold the universal dictionary, which the learned of all nations have opened.)

VIVE LE SPORT!

An English gentleman of breeding was standing face to wall in a dark corner of Paris one night, when a gendarme tapped him smartly on the shoulder, and said:

"Defense de pisser !"

The gentleman replied: "Pardonnez moi M'sieur, je n'pisse pas, je m'abuse.'

"Ah, pardonnez *moi*, vive le sport!"

HE BOOBED!

It was a select Society dinner, and the old waiter was training the young waiter. The great art of the job, he told him, was to be quick in any emergency. . . . "For instance I was on a job at the Palace when a lady with a low blouse and a big chest laughed, and they both popped out. Did I use my bare hands to put them back? no, I. . . ." Here they were interrupted.

The dinner went on, and the young waiter noticed a Peeress with a large chest, a low dress and a hearty laugh. He hung around expecting the worst, and sure enough it happened! Quick as a flash he seized a large serving spoon, and popped them back.

When he rejoined his boss round the back, he said:

"How about that eh? Not bad for a learner?"

"Young man, when you really know the trade you will use a *warm* spoon."

ON THE JOB

A pukka sahib was entertaining the Governor's party; and his wife, in spite of warnings, wore a low dress. Sure enough, in the middle of dinner, there was a calamity when the lady's large bubs flopped out. The husband, quick as a flash, caused a diversion by pointing out of the big window to the lawn, on which was a newly installed fountain:

"I say, look at that splendid sight will you."

They all looked.

A pair of monkeys were coupling on the fountain.

FAMILY TRADITION

A middle-aged colonel left the Indian army and in accordance with his family's tradition, married a young woman. Nine months later he engaged the best Harley Street obstetrician. . . . "See about my son."

"How do you know it'll be a son?"

"It will, family tradition."

When the doctor rang through, it was a son.

"Circumcise him," said the father, against all the doctor's protests, "it's family tradition."

Later the doctor rang and said the child seemed ill. . . .

"Give him a stiff brandy, I'm paying, don't argue."

The doctor rang yet again, and said the child was no better: "Then put him to the breast; I'll come over."

Sure enough, when the father arrived the child was feeding well, and was obviously a very fit baby indeed.

"Splendid," shouted the colonel "there's a real father's son for you, belly full of brandy, mouth full of tit and a sore cock!"

APING HIS BETTERS?

Two old cavalry colonels were talking about a third. . . .

"I say, Smithers old chap, did you hear about Jenkins?"

"No, what's that devil up to now?"

"You'll never believe this old boy, but Jenk has started living in sin with a monkey!"

"By jove! I say what! Male monkey or female monkey?"

"Dammit Smithers, don't say that. Female monkey of course, nothing unnatural about old Jenkins."

PINCHED

The Deb gave a snooty party, and hired a maid, just to show off. Alas, the maid was not really experienced. A second party was organised, and when the Agency sent the same girl along, the Deb said:

"Look here Mary, don't forget the sugar tongs this time: it's not very nice when the men go in the loo, and they take themselves out, and they put themselves back, and then they have to pick up the sugar lumps with their fingers."

The girl swore she would remember this time, but, after the guests had gone, the Deb said: "Mary I thought I told you about the sugar tongs!"

"I put them out My Lady, I swear I did!"

"Well, *I* didn't see them on the table!"

"On the table? My Lady, I should think not, I put them in the toilet."

WHO WOULDN'T?

The Master of an Oxford College invited a well-known public figure to dine at High Table with him, and laid on the best old port for the occasion. Now the visitor was a "temperance" bigot, and when the Master said:

"Will you have some port Sir?" gave the reply:

"By the lord harry! I'd rather commit adultery than drink a single glass of port."

"Who wouldn't?!" said the Master.

SAILOR'S HORNPIPE

An Admiral of the Fleet was a widower, so he sent his daughter to an exclusive and rather narrow boarding school. To his horror, when her education was finished she began courting a common sailor. She waited until she was of age, and then announced that she would marry the Jack Tar. The day before the wedding, the Admiral took his daughter aside, and said:

"This is very difficult for me, in fact I'd rather face the enemy in battle than talk to you about the Facts of Life, but the truth is, well, you see, it's like this, sailors spend months at sea, and they sometimes get peculiar habits, or, er, let me put it this way, if he ever demands sex in a funny way, you tell me and I'll speak to him."

"A funny way father, what exactly d'you mean?"

"Well er, if he er, ever wants it the other way round."

The girl left it at that, and was soon married and on honeymoon. For months she bloomed, then one night going to bed, she said to her sailor husband:

"Jack, have you ever thought you'd like to try sex 'the other way round' whatever that means?"

"What! and fill the bloody house with kids!"

THROUGH THE HOOP

The circus came, and as a treat the nuns were given a block of seats. Most of all they enjoyed the clown. Alas, a great fire broke out in the "big top" and everybody fled for their lives, except one young nun who was a cripple. The clown, with great courage, went into the smoke, and brought her out on his back, which was virgin on the ridiculous!

THE BITER BIT

The Noble Lord and the Noble Lady were middle aged and not on good terms. In fact Her Ladyship was convinced that he was carrying on with the pretty housemaid, so she laid a trap: she suddenly sent Mary home for the weekend.

That night when they went to bed, His Lordship came the Old Story: "Excuse me my dear, my stomach," and promptly disappeared. Her Ladyship promptly dashed along the corridor, up the back stairs, into the maid's bed. She just had time to switch the light off, when in he came. . . .

. . . He wasted no time or words, but quickly took his will. He was still panting when Her Ladyship switched on the light and said: "You didn't expect to find me in this bed, did you?"

"No indeed, Madam," said James, the Butler.

CAME TOO SOON

Mrs Kaysor-Bondor was dressing for a very Grand Occasion, but as she put on her expensive nylons, one laddered. She put on a fresh pair, but they laddered leaving the house; yet another pair went as she entered the car. Her husband was furious. . . . "You're not going back AGAIN! We're late already!"

She replied: "It would never do for Mrs Kaysor-Bondor to appear in laddered stockings, what *would* people think?"

He replied: "Listen, the last big 'do' I went to, that charming Mrs Rendels was there, *and* her four children!"

WITHOUT A.I.D.

The Squire and his Lady were Chief Patrons of the Agricultural Show, and after the opening ceremony they dutifully walked round, mixing with the tenants and peasantry, and looking at the exhibits.

But his Lordship spent so much time in the beer tent that her Ladyship wandered off to admire the prize bull. Never was a male animal so splendidly equipped.

"My, but that's a fine beast you have there Giles," she said to the yokel in charge.

"Yes my Lady, he be champion, and father o' champions."

"Go on, tell me all about him."

"Well Mam, this here bull went to stud three hundred times last year."

"Indeed? Well, go over to his Lordship will you, my good fellow, and tell him that there's a bull here went to stud three hundred times in one year, will you."

Giles dutifully trotted up to Squire and gave the message. . . .

"Very interesting indeed," was his comment, "always the same cow, I presume?"

"Oh, no indeed Sir, three hundred different cows."

"Aha, go and tell her Ladyship that, will you."

There was a young lady of Barking Creek
Who had her monthlies twice a week,
Said a man from Working:
"How provoking"
"You'd get no poking so to speak!"

There was an old man of Pagoda
Would not pay a whore what he owed 'er,
"I'll show you!" she said,
And she jumped out of bed,
And peed in his whisky and soda.

There was a young girl of Malacca
Who played with her boyfriend's left knacker,
One night they were tight
And she played with his right –
The b*gger went off like a cracker!

There was an old fellow of Cosham
Who took out his ballocks to wash 'em,
His wife said: "Now Jack,
If you don't put 'em back
I shall jump on the beggars and squash 'em."

From a tart, a young man of Cape Anchor
Caught syph, gonorrhea, clap and canker,
In addition to crabs
And scabs on the tabs,
So he sent her a postcard, to thank 'er.

Feather Pluckers

Three louts were brought before the Beak for "loitering with intent". The first convinced the Court that he had a steady occupation as a "Car Dealer" and got off. The second said he was a "Street Trader" and after his Pedlars License had been produced, he too was dismissed. The third had to do some quick thinking, and recalled that he had sometimes helped the Market people to get their Christmas poultry ready. . . .

"Your occupation or employment?" said the Beak.

"Sir, I'm one of those what they call, you know, er, feather pluckers. . . ."

"Clever WHAT?"

JUST A MINT

A Banker went up the West End for a night, picked up a tart and asked the price. She told him not to worry, it would be reasonable. After a good night out, she asked for fifty pounds.

"Fifty pounds! far too much!"

"Surely you've heard of me, Polly, the dearest in the game."

"What did you say your name was – Polo?"

"No, silly, Polly. Why Polo?"

"Well you've certainly got a hole with a mint in it!"

THE TACTFUL PLUMBER

The plumber impressed on his new apprentice that tact was essential on the job. "For instance" he said, "I was once following a pipe through a house and I walked into an unlocked bathroom, and there was a woman stark naked. Quick as a flash, I said: "Excuse me, Sir," and went away – "that's tact see."

The next job they went on, the plumber started in the kitchen and sent the kid upstairs to look for the tank. There was a disturbance, and the boy re-appeared with a black eye and a bleeding nose.

"What the hell have you been up to?"

"It's all your fault, you and your bloody tact. There was a courting couple stark naked on a bed upstairs, doing things, and I said: "Excuse me, gentlemen."

HIGHLAND FLING

There was an elocution master went to a ball, and seemed to be getting on famously with a young woman he had picked up.

After a while he said: "You're Scottish, aren't you?"

"How did ye knaw that?" she said.

He replied: "I could tell by the way you roll your R's."

"Nae, nae" she said, "that's just th'effect o' my high heels!"

A man went to his solicitor and said: "I am very rich, so money is no object, but I want to be rid of my wife, who is a bitch, without being had for murder, so tell me what to do."

"Buy her a strong horse and it may throw her."

A month later the man came back and said his wife was now the best horsewoman in the district. . . .

"Try" said the lawyer, "buying her a mini and send her up the M 1 in it."

The man did this, but she drove like Stirling Moss, putting in danger everybody but herself. The husband told the solicitor he was desperate. . . .

"Buy her a big Jaguar."

The man was back in a week delighted. "Name your fee," he said, "it worked!"

"What happened then?"

"Well, when she opened the cage door to feed the jaguar, it bit her bloody head off!"

ON THE MARK

Two old friends went on honeymoon together, and had a bet who would perform the most times first night. It was a point of honour to tell the truth, and each would chalk up his score outside the bedroom door. Jack performed three times altogether, and chalked them up thus: 1 1 1 .

Bill staggered along at breakfast time to see the state of the parties, observed the marks, and said:

"Cor blimey, one hundred and eleven, beat me by two!"

AS YE RAPE, YE SHALL SEW

A man had just done five years in prison for a double rape, and was being discharged. Said the warder: "Here's your civvies, here's the £50 you came in with, sign for them and be off."

As the man departed the warder added: "I suppose you'll be up the West End tonight, looking for a woman."

"A woman? Me? Don't be daft, I've been impotent all my life."

"Impotent? Don't talk like a bloody fool, how can you be impotent when you've just done time for raping two women?"

"I know, I know," said the convict, sadly, "I think I didn't have a very good solicitor."

REDUCIO AD ABSURDAM

A woman complained to her solicitor that every time she had intercourse with her husband it hurt her past all bearing, "He's enormous, simply enormous," she added.

The solicitor said: "In that case madam, the best thing you can do is to file your petition."

"Oh, certainly not! Let him sandpaper his. . . ."

NO CHANGE OUT OF HIM

A man in full morning dress was descending the steps of the Strand Law Courts when a blowsy made-up blonde asked him if he felt like a bit.

"Madam," he replied very haughtily, "permit me to inform you that I am the Crown Solicitor."

"That's quite alright me old cock! I'm the half-crown solicitor!"

PERILS OF POLYGAMY

A Chief in darkest Africa sent his son and heir to London to be educated. The boy divided happy days between classrooms and the West End, until he got a sudden call to go home and take over – his father had suddenly died. Of one thing he was quite certain, he was going to take home an English, king-sized double bed (the like of which he had not previously seen), to accommodate a King Size harem.

All the tribe turned out to see their new ruler, as he arrived accompanied by massive packing cases. As soon as formalities were concluded he ordered the bed to be erected in the Royal Kraal, but here arose trouble. Much of the space was occupied by an enormous ancestral throne made of logs:

"Take that thing outside" said the youth, but at this point a terrible wail arose from the Witch Doctor, who pointed out that for time out of mind it had been known that should the throne leave the Kraal, the Royal Line must die out. After a good deal of argument the boy agreed to leave it in, but to make room for the King Size royal bed, he had the throne lashed to the rafters with primitive ropes.

For a time all went very well, but alas, the insects which lived in the straw roof came out and nibbled at the ropes. One night, when the young Chief was in bed with four of his favourite wives, the throne came crashing down, and killed the lot of them.

PEOPLE WHO LIVE IN GRASS HOUSES SHOULDN'T STOW THRONES!

LOOPING THE LOOP

There was a certain lass who had more bust than brains and she was what is known as a P.T. or "teaser".

It was her custom to go out with men, get her drinks and entertainment paid for, and then "cry off" when the chap claimed his reward.

One day she met her match; he was a sportsman who had a big old saloon car with a useful-sized back seat, and here he was up before the Court charged with rape.

The Chairman of the Bench looked over his glasses at the peroxide blonde in the witness box and said: "But my dear, there wasn't a mark on you – why didn't you struggle in the car?"

"I couldn't!" said the girl, "you know those loops in the corners? Well, he stuck one of my legs through one loop, and the other through the other loop, and there I was, fixed."

"Remarkable, remarkable" said the Beak, "now I know what those loops are for, I often wondered."

"Yes, yes," put in his fellow magistrate, another ancient man, "and what a sign of progress too!"

"Progress? What the blazes are you on about, progress?"

"Why yes, progress my dear Chairman, when I was a young feller there was nothing like that, we had to make do with winding down each window, shoving her foot out and winding it up again."

PENNIES FROM HEAVEN

To the Council of a country town was elected an old farmer, determined to "reduce the rates". When the Surveyor's report was read, it included a scheme to bridge the local stream. "Disgraceful!" shouted the old man, "bridge that! Why I could piss across it."

"You're out of order, completely out of order," bellowed the Mayor.

"Aye, I knows I am, or I could piss twice as far as that."

Later on came a proposal to have a urinal in the market place. "I'm dead agen that," said the farmer, "I move rejection!"

"Shut up you fool" whispered his companion, "we've got to have somewhere to have a run-out."

"Oh, is that what it is? Sorry, Mr Mayor, I withdraw my objection, in fact I move we have an arsenal as well."

A SHINING LIGHT

There was a policeman on night duty who thought he heard something up an entry. He shone his torch up, and observed a young woman with her blouse undone and her knickers round her ankles, calmly eating from a bag of crisps. . . .

"Hey, what's going on there?"

The girl looked up, chewing, and said:

"Blimey! Has he gorn?"

DESIGNING WOMEN

Two men in a London Professional Men's club got into a heated argument as to who had originally designed woman. The architect said only an architect could have designed such beauty, the sweeping curves leading the eye to the essentials, all in perfect proportion ... etc."

"That's all piffle, not to say balls and codswallop," said the engineer: "Woman is functional from first to last, ideally designed to reproduce the race, clearly the work of a skilled engineer."

Finally they referred the matter to the arbitration of a fellow clubman, a retired judge. He thought for a while, then he said:

"You are both wrong, woman was designed by a 'planner' without any doubt."

"How do you make that out?" they both wanted to know.

"Why because only a planner would have placed the pleasure gardens between the Waterworks on one side, and the Sewage Disposal Plant on the other.

STIFF WORK

A young man owned a small and ancient open tourer with a tired engine. One day he took a hefty girl out for a ride in the country, and when they arrived at a remote and steep hill, the car spluttered and finally stopped.

"Shall we get out and push it up?" said the man to the girl.

"A good idea that, but will it be alright to leave the car here?"

NIGHT "MARE"

Twins had been told of the coming of a new baby. As it was due near their birthday, mother, along with the Facts of Life, had also built it up as her additional birthday present to them. And, great joy, the baby did arrive on their birthday and was much loved. Came the next year, and the mother asked the twins what they wanted for a present. They didn't know, so she gave them time to think it over. They came back and said:

"If it wouldn't blow you up too much, do you think you could manage a pony this year?"

HIAWAFFLE

A certain young man was articled as a Civil Engineer, but he could not pass his exams because the Theorem of Pythagorus beat him time after time. In despair he ran away to sea. He deserted ship in the USA, and wandered across the continent. Months later, ragged and hungry, he drifted into an Indian reservation, where they took him in and nursed him back to health. One day he told the Chief the whole story, and the Chief said:

"Our Medicine Man, heap wise, him solve this one."

The Medicine Man listened gravely, and said:

"Paleface, a Brave takes three squaws, one sleeps on a buffalo's skin and has papoose, another sleeps on sheep's skin and has papoose, the third sleeps on hippopotamus's skin, and has twins, what does that prove?"

"Why" said the youth, "it proves the squaw on the hippopotamus's equals the sum of the squaws on the other two's hides."

"Precisely!" said the Medicine Man.

DIRTY WEEKEND

The chemist impressed upon the new boy that in business, politeness was everything. "It doesn't matter if they only come in to ask what time it is, courtesy costs nothing, always be friendly and polite."

With which the chemist departed to have his lunch. When he came back the boy was in a shocking state, with two black eyes and his clothes torn. "It's all your fault, you and your daft advice, look what it's done for me."

"Why, what happened?" said the boss.

"Well, a courting couple came in, arm in arm, and the girl bought a packet of S.T.'s. I remembered what you said, and while I was wrapping them up I politely remarked:

"It looks like being a dull weekend, Sir."

"MISS" UNDERSTOOD

An Oxford student off for a weekend at a country house party arrived at this rustic town realising he had left part of his luggage behind. He went into the only chemists shop in the place, a real old-fashioned pharmacy, and rapped boldly on the counter. The chemist's wife, a right battleaxe, appeared from the back and said: "Yes?"

"Three french letters, Miss," said the young man in loud clear tones.

"Don't you dare 'Miss' me," said the old matron.

"Oh, sorry, four french letters, please."

YOU'RE ALL WRONG, JACK

Two broken-down unemployed actors thought they were certain of a job in the pantomime season, but all the Agent could offer was the cow, in Jack and the Beanstalk. They were hungry, so swore they'd done the part before. "You'd better be good" said the Agent as he threw the skin at them, "we open next week."

To get some practice they went into the country at dawn, and wore the cow's skin up and down in a field. Then the one at the front, who could see, said: "Jack can you run fast?"

"I'll be b*ggered if I can run at all!"

"You'll be b*ggered if you can't, there's a bull coming up behind us."

SHE HAD A CLUE!

A sweep's wife used to bath him every Saturday, but one time when he came in late she set about him with the bathbrush and half killed him.

"What's all this in aid of?" he groaned.

"Always before you've been home at 12 a hundred percent black, now you're home at two, one percent white."

UNREELED HIS HOSEPIPE

A ladder was placed against the bedroom window of a burning house, and a young fireman rushed up. Inside was a curvy brunette in a see-through nightie.

"Aha," said he, "you're the second pregnant girl I've rescued this year!"

"But I'm not pregnant."

"You're not rescued yet."

MANHOLE COVERS

An old railway driver went into a chemists shop and said he had some heavy parcels, would they give him a hand. The chemist went out, read the label, picked up the box, and said:

"I'm an old man, like you, but dammit I can carry a box of ST's without yelling for assistance."

"Blimey!" said the old van driver, "they said at the depot they was manhole covers."

". . . HOW MUCH IT IS"

Two Frenchmen landed in England on a pleasure trip, were told that English girls required a sheath to be used. Not knowing English, the first entered a chemists, put his member on the counter, and a shilling beside it. The other thought that was not enough, so he placed his member on the counter with a florin beside it.

The chemist came out, looked, placed his own member on the counter, picked up the money and walked away.

OF MICE AND MEN

A women entered the chemists and shyly asked for some condoms. The chemist showed her several sizes, but she said they were all too big. Finally he found some dwarf-sized – they were still too big.

"Pardon me Madam," he said, "but your husband seems to be rather, er, ill blessed."

"*My Husband!* Oh you insolent man, we're over-run with mice!"

GROUNDSHEETS, TROOPS, FOR THE USE OF

An ATS driver, after a long journey across Salisbury Plain, arrived at her destination, a remote camp, at midnight.

The Sergeant of the Guard showed her where to leave the lorry, and then said: "Where will you sleep tonight?"

The girl explained that the only thing she could do was to kip down in the cab. It was a cold night, and the Sergeant thought for a moment and said:

"If you like you can have my bunk, I'll sleep on the floor." The offer was accepted with thanks.

After the girl had turned in, she felt very sorry for the Sergeant lying down there on the hard cold floor, and, leaning out, said:

"This isn't right, why don't you get up here and squeeze in alongside of me?" This being done, the "sarge" said: "Well how's it to be? Do you want to sleep 'single' or 'married'?"

The girl giggled and said: "I think it would be nice if we slept 'married', don't you?"

"Right, I'm not fussy, we'll sleep 'married' then," he said, turning his back on her and going off to sleep.

MILITARY MANŒUVRES

There were three ATS girls . . .
The first gave her discharge to an Officer,
The second jumped over a campfire and got deferred,
The third (a driver) swerved to avoid a child,
(and fell out of bed!)

DAUGHTER OF THE REGIMENT

There was an old Colonel who in his middle age suddenly married a young and beautiful girl, in the hope, as he told people, of starting a family.

However, some time went by and nothing happened. Then one day he suddenly paraded the whole regiment:

"Officers, non-commissioned officers, and men of the Thirtyninth Royal Loamshires, I have called you together to make a special announcement: This morning my wife gave birth to a fine girl weighing eight pounds; Officers, non-commissioned officers, and men, of the Thirtyninth Royal Loamshire Regiment, I thank you, one and all."

YOU'LL CARRY THE BANNER

There was once a young woman joined the A.T.S. and went for her "medical". The doctor had her stripped off, and then called over his assistant. "Look at that, the biggest navel I've ever seen in all my career!"

The young doctor looked, and said: "By George girl, that's a huge navel, can I take a photograph of it for the medical press?"

The girl was fed up, and could not understand what all this was in aid of: "You'd have a big navel if you'd been in the Salvation Army for as many years as I have."

This only heightened the mystery: "The Salvation Army, what's that got to do with it?"

"I carried the banner for ten years."

WHORTICULTURE

A Parks Director from the West Country was up in London for a big conference. He went up town at night and picked up a girl. He told this girl that if she would look after him for a week, entertain him, and show him all the hot spots, she should be well rewarded.

At the end of the week this Parks Director told the girl that never in all his life has he had such a wonderful time. Her reward, he said, should be exceptional, for he had succeeded in growing a perfect black rose, which, as soon as he announced the news, would become an international sensation. He would name the rose after her.

She said she'd rather have fifty pounds in cash, thank you.

Which only goes to show, that you may take a horse to water but you can't take a horticulture.

SWEET VIOLETS

An old navvy went into a chemists shop and said: "I want some arse paper" to the sweet young woman behind the counter. The chemist was furious, and he followed the chap into the street: "Look here you!" he said, "we don't mind your custom, but we won't have that language to young lady shop assistants, see."

"I'm on'y an ignorant navvy, what should I a' said?"

"Why 'toilet paper' of course, and remember!"

A week later he came back and said: "I want some soap."

"Yes sir," said the girl with a sweet smile, "toilet soap?"

"Don't be daft miss, I on'y want to wash my hands and face."

There was a young sailor named Guest
Who was struggling to get on the nest,
Said his young Chinese wanton
Don't forget you're in Canton
The tram lines all run East to West!

There was a young man of Devizes
Whose balls were of two different sizes,
One was so small
It was no use at all
While the other took several prizes!

There was an old farmer named Pitt
Whose cart a large boulder did hit
The load of manure
Was so insecure
He was up to his neck in the sh*t!

There was a gym mistress of Munich
Whose muscular action was unique
She wrestled with men
Again and again
And burst all the seams of her tunic!

There was a young lady named Gluck
Who suffered some terrible luck,
Stripping off in a punt
She fell off the front
And was pecked in the dunt by a cuck!

All trains to Aldershot

An old railway servant had spent his whole life at one station on the (former) Great Western line. One of his main jobs was to call out:

"Next train for Oxshott, Aldershot and Bagshot."
"Change for Uppingham, Woking, and Buckingham," not for Hants, Dorset and the West."

One day the District Manager came, and explained that under the Beeching reforms he would be replaced by a Tannoy system, and was now redundant.

On the old man's last day at work, startled commuters heard:

"Next train for Ox sh*t, pig sh*t and all the sh*t."
"Change for tupping'em, poking and *uckingham, not your pants, corsets and vest."
"Furthermore, rollocks, pollocks and asholes to the fornicating railway, I've had me cards!"

A SOFT ANSWER – ON TOILET PAPER

An old miner suddenly won £20,000 on the pools, and told his wife he would never again go down the pit. She insisted he ought to send in a proper letter of resignation, and after much argument he took pen and paper, and wrote:

"Dear Coal Board, – you can keep your lousy, poxy, clapped-up mucking job, and put it where the monkey put the nut. Tell the Overman to stuff my tools up his dirt-box while you're at it.

Yours Truly,
Wm. Bloggs."

"PS: Insulting letter to follow – W.B."

AFTER MANY EXERTIONS

There was a man rushed into a small-town newspaper office in a great state of excitement, and said to the counter clerk:

"Quick, I want to put something in the paper, marvellous! what d'you think, after ten years my wife's had a baby, a fine son, fabulous. . . ."

"Yes, Sir," said the clerk, calmly, when the caller stopped for breath – "How many insertions?"

"Oh, we lost count – bloody hundreds!"

A SITTING TARGET

In the Black Country it is common for the cottage gardens to run down to the canal, with a privy sitting on the edge. Young Albert pushed the privy into the water one night, for devilment. . . .

"Albert, did you push that closet in the cut last night?"

"No, Dad, I didn't do it."

Father tried the friendly approach, and told the boy about George Washington, who cut down the cherry tree, and then owned up, thus escaping dire punishment.

"Now you young beggar, own up, did you push that closet in the cut last night?"

"Father, I cannot tell a lie, I did it."

At which the old man gave his son the hiding of a lifetime.

"Here!" said the kid, sobbing, "you said as how when young George owned up, his dad let him off for telling the truth."

"Listen here you young beggar, when young Washington cut that tree down, his father wasn't sitting in the branches!"

COME TO THE FAIR

During the last war, a farmer was sent a young and pretty Land Girl. He lived with his two sons, his wife being dead, so he thought it wiser to fix the girl up in a small empty cottage on the other side of the farm.

After supper on the day she arrived, he told his younger son, who he thought he could trust, to take the girl home, and come straight back. But the boy returned after midnight, which upset the old man. Next time, he told the older son to see the girl home, and behave himself, but he came home at two a.m.

By now the farmer was worried, and feeling he owed a duty to the girl, although his legs were bad, he decided that he personally would take her home that night. He didn't get back until breakfast time!

The sons teased him unmercifully. . . .

"But father, you'll admit she's pretty?"

"Aye indeed."

"And father, isn't she passionate?"

"Aye, pretty she be, passionate she be, but above all, she's patient!"

PUBLIC RIGHT OF WAY?

There was a Squire's daughter who went to a country Solicitor and complained that a man had put his hand on her leg, and she wanted a prosecution.

This put the lawyer in a spot, because this girl was notorious for scandalous conduct at hunt balls and the like, and the local Bench would react accordingly. The old man stroked his beard, and said:

"Look here, are you sure it was his hand, and not his foot?"

"Hell no, don't be bloody stupid, of course it was his hand."

"What a pity, what a pity, if it had been his foot, we could have run him for trespass."

BLACK SHEEP IN THE FAMILY WAY

A farmer said to his man, "Hodge go down and plough up the old pasture behind the hill, and don't waste any time."

At the end of the day the farmer went to inspect progress, and was pleased to see the pasture all nicely ploughed save for one bit about six by three. . . .

"Hey Hodge, why've you missed this bit?"

"Sorry Master, I can't possibly plough yon, for sentimental reasons, never ask me gaffer, I can't do it."

"Sentimental reasons, what are you on about you girt lout?"

"Well Master, that bit o' grass there was where I had my first experience o' sex."

"Oh, I see Hodge, that's where you first had sex."

"Yes Gaffer, and her mother were looking at us, though that hole in the hedge there."

"Good Lord! Her mother saw you! What did she say?"

"Oh, nothing only just, baa baa ba-a-aa."

UP AND COMING

A farmer complained to the Vet that his stock were not breeding, so the Vet said: "Don't worry, I'll make up a sack of stuff that'll get them going, send your man for it." So the man was sent, but returning, he carelessly ripped the sack on some wire; the stuff was trailed across the fields, and a month's supply instantly consumed.

That evening, Hodge rushed in, shouting: "Master, Master, the goat's doing the sow, the cock's doing the ducks, the bull's doing the mare. . . ."

"Don't stand there like a fool – get out and throw some cold water over them!"

"I can't the donkey's doing the pump."

SUCK IT AND SEE

There was a farmer whose best sow was not at all well, so he consulted the Vet.

Said the Vet: "No real trouble, I'll give you a pessary to put up its backside, that'll put things right."

"And how the heck do I get it up its backside," said the farmer.

"Not to worry, there's a little plastic tube comes with the outfit, you simply insert and blow it up."

When the farmer got home he was late for dinner, so he said to his man: "Take this tube, and blow this pessary up Bluebell's backside."

Half an hour later Hodge was still puffing and blowing, but with no success. The farmer came out and said: "Here! give it to me" with which he reversed the tube, re-inserted it, and blew the pessary up first time.

"Master, master," said Hodge, "why did you turn the tube round?"

"Why did I turn the tube round? Well, I wasn't going to suck the end that had been in your dirty mouth!"

SHE LET THE BOROUGH SURVEY'ER?

A Deb who had a sudden yen to work with sweaty animals applied for a job on a farm, and got herself an interview.

The old farmer showed her the sheep and she said: "What nice pigs." He showed her the hens and she said: "What nice ducks," and this went on all over, so great was her ignorance.

Finally he showed her his prize bull, who was wonderfully equipped, and she said: "What a sweet mare."

"Gore dammee wench! When didst see a mare wi' a pair o' barls loike to yon? Ther never was such!"

"Oh yes indeed" said she, with a sweet smile: "The Mayor of Nuneaton."

GOING TO FOCUS

Two Black Country girls on holiday at Blackpool were walking along the front when one of these beach photographers stepped forward. . . .

"Stand still a minute, Mary, he's going to focus."

"What, both on we?"

NIGHT WORK IF YOU CAN GET IT

It was Friday afternoon, and the foreman told Enoch he'd have to work overtime, so Enoch asked his mate to call home and tell the missus.

Accordingly, Ziah called at the cottage and said:

"Your old man aint coming home until late, how about a bit o' love upstairs?"

The shocked young wife became less shocked when he offered her five pounds, but she still would not.

"Ten pounds then?"

"Er, no."

"Fifteen pounds then."

"Er, well no, it wouldn't hardly be right, would it."

"Come on my wench, fifteen pounds just for half an hour on the bed, and Enoch'll never find out!'

She needed no more persuading, but took him in the bedroom, giving due value for money.

When the husband came home late, he said:

"Did my mate tell you I'd be working over?"

"Yes, duck, he called in for a minute."

"Oh, and I suppose he handed you my wages like I asked him."

A SHAGGY DOG

A countryman went into a London pub with a dog. The man ordered a pint, the dog ordered a whisky.

"What the hell!" said the barman.

"Yes," said the owner, "he's the most intelligent dog in the West Country; I brought him to see the sights of town."

"If I give him fivepence, will he get me a paper?" said the barman, "because I forgot to get one."

"Of course I will," piped up the dog, then, receiving the money, "back soon, tat ta."

The dog did not return, so, after an hour, the worried owner went in search. He finally found his dog in a back alley, nicely on the job with a bitch.

"Well I'm damned!" said the owner, "you've never done that before."

"No," said the dog "I've never had the money before."

UP AND DOWN ALONG

A yokel married the curviest girl in the village, and she was also the dimmest.

He took her to a little cottage after the wedding, and soon after dusk he had her upstairs, in bed, and on the job.

After a repeat performance he excused himself, left the bedroom, but returned in five minutes to perform again.

This happened about six times more, after which the girl protested:

"George, you be going to the lavatory a terrible lot o' times tonight!"

To which she got the reply:

"I ain't George. George is downstairs taking the half-crowns."

THE SODS HAVE GONE

In a council house lived a man who went to much trouble growing a front lawn from seed. The day came when he had got a better job in another town, and in putting his notice in, he told the rent collector he was going to take the lawn with him.

When this was reported to the Council, they took a poor view of it, holding that as the soil in the garden was theirs, the lawn must be theirs. The row became public, and the Town Clerk told the rent collector to watch the position very closely.

One day the Clerk found a note on his desk which read:
"The sods have gone."
He sent one back:
"Yes, but what's become of the lawn?"

MUCKING ABOUT WITH LANGUAGE

A woman had a daughter who began to bring home a "superior" bank clerk. Father insisted on showing the superior young man his garden, which was a very fine one. . . .

"Sir, how d'you get such lovely roses?"

"Muck, young man, muck."

"And that superb rhubarb?"

"I does it wi' muck. Lots and lots on it. Muck on the taters, muck on the cabbages, muck on everything."

Afterwards the daughter took her mother on one side and said: "Can't you please get father to use a more respectable word than 'muck' when somebody decent comes to the house?"

"My dear girl! It's taken me 25 years to get him to say 'muck'."

A RATTLING GOOD STORY

Two Portsmouth prostitutes picked up two sailors, and each took one home for the night.

They met the next day and compared notes:

"How'd yer get on, Mabel?"

"Nicely thank you, Mary, he had it three times, gave me fifteen pounds, and helped wash up after breakfast. How about you?"

"Terrible, terrible! Never gave me a moment's rest all night, stuck an old-fashioned pop bottle up my fanny, and cleared off without paying!"

"You were a bit slow, why didn't you take out the pop bottle and hit him on the head with it?"

"I didn't know it was there until I heard the marble rattling as I was coming down the stairs this morning."

WORSE THAN DEATH?

There was a Irish village girl left home for the great lights, and returned home loaded with money and finery.

"Is it indade a great good job yez have in London thin?" enquired her mother. The girl wouldn't say what the job was, but after much badgering she whispered in her mother's ear. The old lady shrieked, groaned and fainted right off.

When they'd brought her round she asked: "Whit's that ye said ye wuz agin?"

The girl told her.

"Arrahh, praise be to arl the saints! Oi thought at first ye said ye'd become a *protestant.*"

ONE OF OURS

The Irish navvies were digging the road outside a house full of made-up floozies. A parson came along, pulled down his hat and went in. Says Pat to Mike:

"Did you see that! Just what you'd expect with one of them parsons!" Soon after a rabbi arrived, turned up his collar, and in he went. Says Mike to Pat: "Is it not a terrible thing that the priest of God's Own People should go in there!"

Lastly a Catholic priest arrived, wrapped his cloak round his head, and dived quickly into the bawdy house.

"Pat, isn't that dreadful now, to think that one o' the girls must have been taken ill."

LITTLE BY LITTLE

A much married man who had been repressed, won a free holiday, a week in Paris. He asked the porter at the hotel how to get to a brothel. He was told not to worry, just go down Montmatre, and he would find English visitors catered for. Sure enough, he soon found a chap in uniform who said: "You want a sexy girl? Pay at the desk, and follow the signs."

He paid up, and followed an arrow "British this way" leading to doors: "Under ten stone" and "Over ten stone". Thus to: "Under 5 ft 6" and "Over 5 ft 6". Still following directions he came to "Under 50" and "Over 50", and finally: "Under four inches" and "Over four inches".

Opening the appropriate door, the would-be roué found himself back in the street!

THREE-DIMENTIONAL

A six foot, 16-stone, 25-year-old Australian came in from the outback when gold was discovered on his land, and took a plane to London, where he sought the pleasures of the West End, and its well known "ladies".

Unfortunately, although he got many girls as far as the bedroom, one sight of his monstrous member caused one and all to faint, or feign illness. Not even for a hundred pounds would any girl risk damaging her ration book. One night, disconsolate, he was stopped by a girl on the game, who said: "What about it? I've got the smallest, tightest. . . ."

"Listen Marm, that's what I'm *not* looking for," and he explained his difficulty. The little tart said she had many friends in the game, and among them one who could satisfy even this over-endowed cowboy.

The Aussie had his doubts, but the tart said her friend was trained by the USA Army from the age of 12, so off they went in a taxi to Big Fanny's. It was to be £100 for the fee, and £10 for the agent, and in went the agent to tell Big Fanny all about it. The latter came out, and said:

"I fear no man born, come on Aussie, tell me how big it is?"

The Colonial flustered, and finally said:

"Four inches!"

"Four inches! Cripes, you don't call that a man's size do you? Cor what a fuss over nothing!"

"Thick, Marm, thick."

THE LAST OF WAILS

A man who wished to walk in the Welsh mountains made his headquarters at a pub in a country town. He found his evenings dull, for nothing happened and pub conversation was mostly about sheep, mostly in Welsh. He asked the landlord how to set about finding the Ladies of the Town, and that worthy was shocked:

"Look man, this is Wales man, we couldn't have prostitutes, the Chapel would never allow it." The visitor looked sad, and the man continued: "Of course we have human nature the same as anywhere, but the thing you mention is kept out of sight."

He went on to explain that up the mountain at the back were caves, well furnished and with all mod con. What the stranger must do was go up the mountain at dusk and shout "Yoo-oo-hoo" and if the lady yoo-hoo'd back, terms could be negotiated. If she was already engaged, there would be no answer.

That evening the Englishman yoo-hoo'd his way from cave to cave, but with no luck at all. He finally decided to go back and get drunk, but at the foot of the mountain he found a fresh cave.

"Yoo-hoo, yoo-hoo," he shouted.

"Yoo-hoo yoo-hoo-oo-oo-oo," came back so clearly.

He rushed into the cave and was killed by a train.

BOTTOMS UP

This man married the curviest girl in the office, and all his mates envied him. In particular an unmarried young Scot, who said one day: "You ken, I'd give a hundred pounds to smack the pretty bottom of yon wee wife o' yours."

Smith was furious, and went home raging to his wife about it. But the wife had Scots blood too, and she said: "You know the furniture isn't paid for, and I could do with a fur coat, what's a few smacks on the bottom?"

Finally she wore her husband down, and he was forced to tell Jock that it was on for him to smack the wife's bare bottom for a hundred pounds, but only on terms. The husband was to be there, and no funny business.

So the three were in a suburban bedroom, the blushing wife removed her panties and bent over. . . . Jock threw her skirt up and gently stroked her, saying "What beautiful curves, what pinkness, what dimples, what firmness, . . ." and all the time rubbing and stroking, while the husband was nearly in hysterics. When Jock suddenly produced a flash camera and took a photo, the husband yelled, "Get on, get on and smack it, or else the deal's off."

"Och no!" said Jock, "I could not bring myself to smack such a beautiful bottom as this one, and besides, it would cost me a hundred pounds if I did!"

INTENT

Mac was courting a wee girl, and this wee girl had a wee flat, but Mac could never get further than the doorstep. Always he would take her home and say: "Can I come in for a whiles, Mary?"

And always she would reply:

"Nae, nae, Mac, I can see the glint in your eye!"

Mac saw that this glint-in-his-eye business was his undoing, so one night as he took the girl towards her flat, he craftily put on a pair of sun-glasses:

"Can I come in the flat a wee whiles, Mary?"

"Nae, nae, Mac."

"But Mary, you cannot see any glint in my eye!"

"Nae, nae, Mac, but I can see the tilt in your kilt!"

HIS YARDSTICK

Jock's young lady mentioned that her birthday was coming up, and Jock could not think of an inexpensive present. His mother had just finished making him a pair of breeks for wearing under his Sunday kilt, and she remarked that there was a yard of the material left, no-doubt clever Jeannie could make something of it.

Jock thought that was a splendid plan, and when he had taken the girl a walk on the heath, he stopped, spun round fast on his heels until his kilt flew up:

"Jean, did ye see anything?"

She blushed, and said that she had not, so Jock then spun round until his kilt was horizontal, blissfully unaware that he had in fact forgotten to put his breeks on. . . . "Surely Jeannie, ye saw it that time?"

"Aye Jock, I did."

"Well, you're having a yard of it for your birthday."

ODD STORY

An Insurance Agent went into a pub and remarked as he stood at the bar:

"I've just taken over London Road, and do you know, every housewife along there is an easy pushover!"

"Every one?" enquired a bystander who was listening.

"Well, to be exact, all but one."

Now, this bystander lived in London Road and he went home deep in thought, and repeated to his wife what he had just heard.

"... all but one?" echoed his wife.

"All but one!"

"Dear me, I wonder who that can be."

A LONG RIDE

A chap in a sports car picked up a girl and drove into the country. The car began to cough and splutter, and they just managed to get into a lay-by before it conked out.

"Excuse me," said the driver, with which he got out and crawled underneath. He was there some time when the girl called out:

"Can I do anything for you?" to which he replied:

"Yes, come under here, and hold this."

An hour later a lorry driver tapped the young man on the shoulder, and said:

"Excuse me, but your car's been gone a long time."

There was a young lady named Dodd
Who thought that her child came from God
It was not the almighty
Who lifted her nightie
But Roger, the lodger, the sod!

There was a young lady named May
Who purchased a new whirling spray
She said: "Ah, that's better!"
As she washed out a letter,
"It's been there since Victory Day."

Said a young homo twin to his brother:
(When told of the death of their mother)
"Now don't look so sad
"For it isn't that bad –
"After all, we can still have each other."

There once was a Bey of Algiers
Who said to his harem: "My Dears,
"Though you may think it odd o' me,
"I've given up sodomy,
"Tonight we start breeding" – LOUD CHEERS!

There was a young lady named Wallace
Used monkeys and snakes for her solace,
The children had scales
And prehensile tales
And voted for Governor Wallace

Too late my love, Too late my love

A famous old violinist was proud of just two things, his
Stradivarius and his virtuous young wife. They went on a
long sea voyage on one of these cargo boats, and the captain
with whom they dined daily, was much attracted to the
wife. One day he said: "You know, I'd give a hundred
pounds to have your wife in my cabin for an hour." The
violinist replied:

"It wouldn't do you any good, her virtue is proof against
all temptation."

The end of the argument was, that the captain bet his
ship against the "Strad" that if he could have the young
girl in his cabin for an hour, he would conquer. When
everything was signed and sealed, the captain took the
lady to his cabin and quickly pulled the curtains.

The fiddler, very confident up to now, began to panic,
and after ten minutes, crept round and listened at the
ventilator. What he heard alarmed him, and he shouted
down:

Be true my love, be true my love,
Be true for one short hour
Just close your legs, your husband begs
And then this ship is ours!

*   *   *

Too late my love, too late my love,
He's got me round the middle,
He's locked the door, I'm on the floor . . . (Ooh–ow!)
You've lost your bleeding fiddle!

BIG PEAT

The Bishop was lacking in golf practice, and going out on a strange course he removed a fearful divot.

The Professional had warned the caddy, that, going out with a Bishop, he must mind his language most carefully, so when the latter said:

"Where did that little sod go to?" the boy said:

"Over the bleeding hedge, and don't forget, you started it."

NOT CAUGHT BY THE SHORTS

There was a man went to a new district, and being a keen golfer, joined the local club.

"Go in the Club House," said the Secretary, "and get yourself a drink, two if you like, we don't charge new members, first day."

The man had several drinks, and thought perhaps he'd take a lunch before playing. As he'd had the drinks for free, he ordered a blowout, but when he called for the bill, the waiter said: "That's all right, new member, first day."

Off went the man to play, but found he'd not brought any balls, so he went to see the Professional, who gave him six. "By the way," said the Professional, "those balls are £5 each cash down, if you don't mind, Sir."

The man said: "There's one thing about this Club, they don't catch you by the food and drink."

ALL FOR ONE, AND ONE FOR ALL

There was a young married man who was very keen on trade union work, so he was given the job of going to a country town to get a new branch going. About a dozen new members turned up, but, the business taking much longer than was expected, he missed the last train back.

"Never mind," said one chap who had taken him to the station, "come and kip at my place, we'll get you some early breakfast, you can whip off in the morning straight to your office, and no harm done."

All went as agreed, but when the chap got home at night, his wife, who was a jealous bitch, gave him a fearful doi . It was worse when she asked him who he'd sta ed with, because he couldn't remember, as they were all equally strangers. She was convinced he'd been with a wom n

She would not rest, but at the first opportunity searched his drawers, and discovered the list of names and addresses of those who had attended the meeting. Then she wrote to each and every one, demanding: "Did my husband sleep at your house on the night of the 31st?

All twelve wrote back and said: "Yes".

NOT STANDING?

There was a man who was a keen political worker, and when the General Election came along, they asked him to be the Party Agent.

The Vicar met him one day and said: "Moggs, you look terribly depressed, is anything the matter?"

"Yes, indeed, Vicar, I'm having great difficulty in getting my member in."

"Dear me, dear me, have you tried vaseline?"

SWEET VIOLETS

There was a fellow went to a dance, and he was going round the floor with a pretty girl, to whom he said:

"Your name's Rose, isn't it?"

"How did you know?"

"I could tell by the scent you are wearing."

The same thing happened later on with a girl named Violet, again he could tell by the scent she was wearing.

The bystanders however were somewhat startled towards the end of the evening to hear a girl saying to him sharply:

"But how did you know my name was Fanny?"

HIS OLD CHINA

A young chap had to go to London on his firm's business, and he said to his older and more experienced colleague:

"What's the best chance for a bit of fun?"

His mate told him of a private hotel where the special feature was early morning tea brought up by a very voluptuous chambermaid, who could be made agreeable at a reasonable price.

"The hotel's a bit dear, but it's good value, if you see what I mean."

The man made a special point of staying at this place and ordered early morning tea very firmly.

The early morning tea was brought up by an old, scruffy, and unfriendly porter. . . .

"Hey," said the guest, "where's the chambermaid?"

"I've no idea, but the teapot's made in Stoke-on-Trent."

FUNNY BONE

A stranger got into a suburban railway carriage in which two men were already sitting. One of them had a peculiar mannerism, he scratched his elbow again and again.

This elbow-scratching was nearly driving the stranger mad, by the time the victim got out at his station.

"Gravely afflicted, your friend," he said to the other man.

"Yes, indeed, he's got a terrible dose of piles."

"I'm not talking about piles, I'm talking about all that scratching just now."

"Yes, that's right, piles, you see, he's a civil servant, can't tell his arse from his elbow."

SHE'D HAD HER CHIPS

There was a woman went to go on a coach trip, and she had a baby in her arms. The driver said:

"Hey there, missus, no babies allowed on long-distance coaches."

The woman went away, but she was determined to travel, so she wrapped the baby up in a bundle and boarded the next coach.

The driver enquired: "What've you got in that bundle, missus?"

"Just fish and chips," she said.

"Well, you'd better hurry up and eat them, the vinegar's running out."

NINETY-NINE, BONK!

Two gentlemen centipedes were in the King's Road, Chelsea, when they spied a lady centipede.

Says one to the other: "Look, George, there's a nice pair o' legs, pair o' legs, pair o' legs. . . ."

BALLADS TO YOU, TOO!

A man who worked as a humble clerk went along to a Hilton Hotel, and asked if they could use an evening pianist.

"As a matter of fact," said the manager, "I've just heard my regular pianist is ill this week, I can find you a job provided you are a good pianist."

"Anything you can hum, I can play," said the applicant.

"O.K.," said the manager, "there's one other thing, you must wear a dinner suit."

The man explained that his dinner suit was very tatty, owing to lack of engagements lately, but it would be all right if the manager agreed to lower the lights on the stage.

All went according to plan, in fact the pianist played brilliantly, but when the man stood up to receive the applause, the manager was horrified. He dashed on the stage and hissed:

"For cripes sake! Do you know your balls are hanging out?"

"You hum it, I'll play it," was the reply.

OUT IF IN, IN IF OUT

The rent collector told the woman she'd be thrown out if she didn't pay the rent. She explained that she was always in debt through having so many children. . . .

"Whose fault's that?" snapped he, "it must be either you or your husband to blame!"

"Well, I suppose you could say it's 'Sex of one and half a dozen of the other'."

WHAT BRASS!

A dashing man went to a dance where he was unknown, and looked around for a prospect. Across the room he saw what he thought was a very curvaceous piece, so he waved and began to walk over.

As he approached he could see she was by no means pretty, and as he got near he could see she was an elderly gargoyle.

It was too late, she had risen to accept his offer. . . .

Suddenly he saw his escape route: "Pardon me," he said, "but I mistook you for my mother."

"But," she said, "you couldn't possibly have mistaken me for your mother: don't you see, I'm wearing a wedding ring."

ALL FOR THE UNION

The Director of a large motor manufacturing company was walking through his factory when he saw a man and a woman having intercourse on a bench during working hours.

He turned to the manager at his side and said:

"Sack that man at once!"

"We can't do that," said the manager, "he's the shop steward for this section."

"Then sack the woman!"

"You can't do that either, Sir, she's the Convenor's secretary."

"Damn and blast it! I'll show you who gives the orders in this place, take that bench outside!"

THE KEYHOLE IN THE DOOR

A certain mayor and some councillors were leaving the town hall late one night after a function. Somebody noticed a light on in the Medical Officer's room, and they all went over to have a peep.

The mayor's pretty secretary was naked on the floor, and the MoH was on top of her, indulging in social intercourse.

They looked at each other aghast, and one councillor said:

"We must sack the mayor's secretary at once!"

"Certainly not!" said the mayor, "we must sack the doctor."

Somebody protested that the secretary would be a loss, the Medical Officer of Health would be a greater loss . . . and was interrupted by a Scots councillor:

"Could we not," he said, "could we not just buy a wee curtain?"

HOW UNFEELING

There was a medical student went on honeymoon, and a telegram was received and opened by the manager: COME HOME AND GET MARRIED ALL IS FORGIVEN. He made up his mind to have revenge on the man he thought had played this trick, a man by the name of Smith.

Smith was too clever, when he got married he gave a false address, and even hid his car so that it could not be interfered with.

On returning from his honeymoon he met his old tutor, who said: "Smith, you are walking round in a thoughtful and rather grim manner, are you looking for something?"

"Yes, Sir, I'm looking for the gentleman who put local anaesthetic in the vaseline."

THE NAKED TRUTH

A New Zealand city, founded in 1868, was presented by the founder with a pair of statues to stand in the Market square. They were life size, naked, very obviously male and female, and they faced each other a few feet apart for a hundred years.

One night Venus, Goddess of Love, appeared to them and said: "For a hundred years you have faced each other with arms outstretched, I will reward your patience with any one wish, if you ask."

The man replied: "We have only ever had one thought, will you make us human for just 24 hours, so that we may do what we have in mind?"

"At dawn you shall come alive," said Venus.

Accordingly they came alive and rushed into each others arms. . . . "How shall we begin?" said the woman.

"I know!" said the man, "I'll catch the beggars in those cabbage nets, and you pull their necks."

OUTSTANDING DIFFICULTY

A young typist complained that her machine was faulty; it was always making extra spaces in her typing copy. The makers sent mechanic after mechanic, but the defect remained. Finally the boss said: "This is our best customer," and sent the Sales Manager in person.

The Sales Manager sent a wire almost at once: "Solved it" and was back the same day. A delighted Director asked him, how?

"Easy, I simply raised her seat three inches."

BEGGAR YOU JACK

A certain civil servant had a cold wife, three howling kids, and when his mother-in-law came to live with them it was the last straw.

The man fled to Tibet and took refuge in a monastery.

The Head Llama said: "You cannot stay unless you work hard, speak little, and eat less."

The man looked downcast, but he said he would try it.

"Mind you," went on the Llama, "we understand the weakness of men, and when you feel that you can remain celibate no longer, you can have a one-night pass to go up the mountain at the back."

"And what good will that do me, O Blessed Llama?"

"You see my son, on top of the mountain is a yak, and you can spend the night with it. It isn't much, but it makes a break in the long round."

When it was the civil servant's turn, he went up the mountain and had his session with the yak. On returning the Llama said:

"Did you enjoy yourself?"

"Yes, O Blessed One, I took full advantage of the opportunity."

"Good! and of course, you fed and watered the yak, and cleaned out the hut afterwards?"

"No, I certainly did not!"

"Ah just as I thought – the English civil servant – 'b*gger you yak, I'm alright!' "

A LITTLE OF WHAT YOU FANCY

A man who had felt unwell for some time went to his doctor and asked for a check-up. The doctor gave him a going over and said:

"Either you pack up smoking, drinking and sex, or you'll be dead in twelve months."

After a while the man went back and said "Look, I'm so bloody miserable I might just as well be dead, *please* can I smoke just a little."

"Very well, just five filter-tips a day," said the medico, who was a very abrupt man.

Some weeks later the man was back again: "Look here, I do miss my pint, please . . . ?"

"All right, two halves a day then, and no spirits."

Time went by, and the patient approached the doctor for the third time –

"Yes, yes, but only with your wife – no excitement!"

SHE THOUGHT HE WAS A CLOSET

A newly-made Lord Mayor found himself at a big dinner, seated opposite a very well-upholstered dowager; her generous charms were generously exposed, and stuck in the vee-line of her more-than-ample was a rose.

The Lord Mayor found the scenery most distracting, he could not take his eyes off it, and finally, catching the lady's questioning glare, blurted out:

"Madam, I was wondering if you would blush if I plucked your rose?"

In clear ringing tones she replied: "Sir, would you flush if I pulled your chain?"

"A HAND IN THE BIRD'S WORTH . . ."

There was a young chap taking a girl out, and doing pretty well. The girl thought an engagement ring was on the way, but the man left London for a better job in Newcastle. He wrote regularly at first, but then tailed off, and his girl wrote and demanded to know the reason. The reply was:

"Sorry, but I've found a regular girl up here."

To the further question: "What has she got that I haven't got?" came a final note:

"Nothing, but she's got it here."

CORNY JOKE

A young lady mouse lived in a cornfield. One day, just as she was all dressed up to go out and meet her boyfriend, a gigantic machine came along, and mouse nest and all were swept up, bashed, and thrown out again, inside a tight bale.

The mouse, much damaged, managed at last to nibble her way out, and fell at the feet of her boyfriend. She was scratched all over, an ear and part of her tail were missing. . . .

"What on earth's happened to you,?' he asked.

"I've been reaped!"

LOVING CUPS

Two fleas got locked up in a ladies dress shop, and went to sleep in a brassiere.

That's how they became bosom friends.

FED UP, FOULED UP, AND FAR FROM HOME

There was a man in a railway carriage who was joined by another man who had with him a crowd of dirty and ill-behaved kids: before they had gone very far he gave one of his kids a fearful belting.

"Look here," said the other man, "you stop beating that child, or I'll get you into trouble."

"You'll do what?"

"I said: 'I'll get you into trouble.'"

"Listen, my friend . . . my wife has run off with a black man taking every penny I've got; I am on my way to leave these kids with a relative who drinks; the girl in the corner is fifteen, and eight months pregnant, that kid over there has messed his pants, the baby has thrown the flask out of the window, and the one I've just beaten has swallowed our tickets. For being off my work I've had the sack, did you say you were going to get me into trouble?"

BLESS YOU!

A young lady suffering from a cold went to a dance with two handkerchiefs, one in her evening bag and a reserve tucked down the front of her dress. During the course of the evening she finished using the one in her bag and tried to retrieve the second, but she couldn't find it. A gentleman at a nearby table who had been watching with interest was amazed to hear her remark.

"I could have sworn I had two when I came!"

ROCK BOTTOM

A certain man was head of a firm of Industrial Consultants. One night at his Club a member came up whom he knew slightly and said:

"Look here old man, you're an efficiency expert, I wonder if you could help me."

"What's the problem?"

The man explained that he owned a factory making seaside lettered rock, and it was losing money.

The expert went round to the rock factory, cut out overtime, tightened up the piecework system, and installed new time clocks. "In a few months time you'll be rolling in the money," he told the owner.

Not many weeks later the owner was back, looking depressed . . . he was still losing money. So the expert went along, cut out the tea breaks, speeded up the conveyor belts, and again departed.

Two weeks later the owner told him he was calling a meeting of his creditors. . . .

"What's gone wrong old boy?"

"Well, you tell me how I can sell ten thousand sticks of rock with ROTTEN BLEEDER lettered in them."

THE ELASTIC LIMIT

A girl from the factory floor was giving evidence against a youth who had stolen her purse. The Beak listened and said: "But my dear girl, if it was in the top of your stocking, how is it you didn't realise?"

"Oh, Sir, I didn't think it was that he was after."

There was a young lady of Wantage
Of whom the Town Clerk took advantage
Said the Borough Surveyor:
"You'll now have to pay 'er
"You've altered the line of her frontage!"
It was really a female of Thame
Who fled there to cover her shame,
She was heavy with child
And it makes them so wild
That their shortsighted Clerk took the blame

A policeman of Paddington Junction
Whose organ had long ceased to function
All the days of her life
Deceived his poor wife
By the dexterous use of his truncheon

There was a young girl of Malay
Who got put in the family way
By the mate of a lugger,
An ignorant b*gger
Who even spelled quim with a K!

A young man of Aberdeen
Invented a screwing machine
Concave or convex
To suit either sex
And a bucket below for the cream

I am the Vicar

You'll carry the banner tonight!
I don't wanna carry the banner tonight
You'll carry the beggar tonight, TONIGHT!
I'll not carry the banner any night
Then you'll come away to the woods, TO THE WOODS!
I don't wanna go to the woods
You're going to come away to the woods!
But I'm in the family way
You're in every beggar's way!
But I'm only thirteen
I'm not superstitious!
I'll tell the Vicar
I AM the Vicar!

AND THE LITTLE PIECES OVER THERE

It was in the days of unemployment that the little labourer
walked into the yard and asked for a job. "You're in luck,"
said the ganger, "see that great big pile of scrap timber,
well, the gaffer wants the little pieces over there and the
big pieces over there." For two hours he toiled, and had
just finished when the ganger said: "He made a mistake, he
wants the little pieces over *there*, and the big pieces over
there." The little man had just finished, and was going for
his dinner when a further message came, to move them all
back again. Said the man to the ganger:

"I'll tell you what he wants, he wants them up . . .'
(The foreman, a huge hairy fellow, had just walked up
behind, and said:) "Yes, go on, what do I want then?"

"Why, Sir, you want the little pieces over *there* and the
big pieces over *there*."

HIS PENCIL

A girl married a chap, a quiet unpushing sort, a humble clerk. When they had been married a week the man came home rather out of temper and said:

"When I got to work this morning, I found a pencil tied on John Thomas!"

"Yes," she said, "I thought if you couldn't come you could write."

SPREAD THE BLESSINGS

A man took his little lad to the pantomime. They secured seats in the front row of the gods, and as they entered, father said: "Do you want a wee-wee before we settle down?"

The kid swore he did not.

No sooner were they well hemmed in than the lad started off that he must have a wee-wee. Father was furious, and told the boy to shut up until the lights went out. The kid fidgeted no end, but at last the lights went out, and father said: "Go quietly over the front edge."

Quite soon an extremely toffee-nosed voice from the stalls shouted up: "I say you cads, play the White Man, wave it about a bit."

A SHOT IN THE DARK

In the old days of the silent film, every decent cinema had its own orchestra. Then, as now, they were the haunt of courting couples, and this pair were sitting in the dark near the front, having a right good maul.

"Mary," whispered the man, "keep on playing with it and making it bigger."

"All right," said the girl, "if you promise to control yourself, and not make a mess."

The man solemnly promised, but what with the heat, and the X-certificate picture, and one thing and another, he broke his word.

"There!" hissed the girl, "now you've done it, you've come in my hand, whatever shall I do with it?"

"Raise your hand and flip it away."

The girl did as she was bid, and flipped it away.

Down at the front there was another whispered argument, between the conductor and the first fiddle:

"Hey, for cripes sake, you're about three bars late!"

"Well, somebody's come in my eye!"

"I'm not surprised, you've been playing like a twat all night."

NELL'S DILEMMA

Nellie Wallace would rush breathless on to an empty stage and say: "Sorry I'm late folks, but the manager blocked my passage."

A variant was: "I got to the theatre late, I was on one of those cliff walks when I met a man, and I didn't know whether to toss him off or let him block my passage."

A TICKLISH JOB!

An army unit crossing the Western Desert, complete with camel transport. Bombardier Smith had a particularly difficult stubborn camel, which finally stopped altogether. The others pressed on regardless.

Smith was stuck there for hours, trying every trick in the book to make the camel go, but in vain.

An ATS driver came along, and asked what the trouble was, so he told her. "That's easy, leave it to me," she said, and proceeded to put her hands beneath the camel's belly. The camel jumped up, and disappeared at the rate of knots after its long-departed companions.

"What on earth did you do Miss, what's the trick?"

"Quite simple, Bombardier, I simply tickled its balls!"

"By cripes then, you'd better tickle mine quick, I've got to catch the b*gger!"

AND KISS HER BETWEEN THE DRAWS?

There was a clippie on a bus late in the evening, who noticed a boy sitting downstairs and calmly smoking. She thought he was out late anyway, and she said to him: "How old are you?"

"Twelve."

"Twelve, and smoking!"

"Yes."

"What if the Inspector gets on?"

"Well, what if he does?"

"Do you want to get me into trouble?"

"Yes thanks, what time do you finish work?"

SHACKED OUT

A sultan had thirty wives, and they made so much racket he built a special suite for them half a mile from his palace. He kept a strong youth, and whenever he felt like it he would press a bell, and when the youth appeared would say: "Fetch me number 15" or "Fetch me number 37" or whatever the case might be.

The youth would have to run all the way with the message, and such was the sultan's nature that he was kept pretty busy. One day he trotted off with the usual message, but he didn't come back.

The sultan sent out servants to search, and they found the young man dead, from heart failure.

The moral of this story is: It isn't sex that kills a man, but the running about after it.

NOT UP AND COMING

There was a gormless young man going out with a well shaped and sexy girl, but she could make no progress with him. She got him alone in the woods and put his hand in her blouse. He took it out again. She lifted up her skirts to show her knickers, and he talked about the weather.

Finally she stepped out of her pants, thrust her thighs towards him, and said:

"Don't you know what this is?"

"No, I don't, what is it?"

"Why you fool, it's a twat!"

"Oh, how interesting, that's what they call me at work."

CROSS EYED

A man went to his local Health Executive, and asked for a new pair of glasses. The man looked up the record and said: "You only had the last pair a month ago."

"I know," said the man, "but I got them broken in an accident."

The clerk looked up the Book of Words—"Domestic Accident, Road Accident, Accident at Work, . . ." no, it wasn't any of those.

"What was it then?" said the clerk.

"I – I don't like to tell you," stammered the applicant.

"No satisfactory explanation, no new glasses," snapped the clerk, getting fed up.

"Very well then," said the man, "I was kissing my girl."

"How the hell could you break your glasses kissing a girl?"

"You see, she crossed her legs."

WASHED HIS HANDS OF IT

A Frenchman was staying in England, and a friend asked him how he was getting on. He said he was doing very well, except for one thing: "When I go to a party, the hostess, she does not tell me where is the *pissoir*. . . ."

"Ah, Georges, you mean she does not tell you where the toilet is? That's just our English prudery; actually, she will say, 'Do you want to wash your hands?' and that means the same thing."

The Frenchman made a mental note of this, and the next time he went to a party, with the hostess waiting for him, the guests standing around heard: "Good evening Mr Du Pont, do you want to wash your hands?"

"No tank you Madame, I have just washed them up against de tree in de front garden."

IN GLAMORGAN

"Dai, did you hear the news? Megan Evans is getting married."

"Indeed now, I did not even know she was pregnant!"

"Steady there Dai, Megan Evans is not pregnant."

"What! Getting married and not even pregnant, bloody middle-class snobbery, that's what that is!"

UP AND DOWN

A courting couple were out walking and could not find a privy place to start petting in. At last they came to a gentleman's park with a high wall all round it; just the job, only the girl couldn't climb the wall.

"Here, stand on this," said the man, producing from his trousers a splendid specimen of manhood.

"No fear! How will I be able to get back?"

V.G. OR V.D.?

There was a courting couple out in the country and they entered a wood and lay down under some bushes. Very shortly afterwards they heard the tramp tramp of marching feet; a squad of troops just back from the Near East was coming along the nearby road: "Company, halt! Fall out for five minutes," at which dozens of soldiers entered the woods and began to relieve themselves all over the place.

The girl watched fascinated through the leaves, and after the soldiers had fallen into their ranks again, and departed, she said:

"George, I suppose those were the officers, those who had theirs wrapped in cotton wool?"

OOMPAH OOMPAH, STUFF IT UP YOUR. . . .

An Arabian Oil Magnate sent for a famous dance band from England, to go and play before his courtiers, harem, etc, and this was arranged.

The band played their best, the Magnate was delighted. He clapped his hands and said:

"Let their instruments be stuffed with gold pieces."

All were delighted except the poor old flautist, whose instrument was too small in diameter to take even one gold piece.

Next night they played again, but the Magnate had got indigestion, and he shouted: "Seize them, and let their instruments be stuffed up their. . . ."

Again the flautist was the unlucky one.

CURTAINS!

Says Mum to Dad: "Those two are very quiet in the front room, go and see what's going on." Dad went through, came back, said nothing, and resumed his paper.

Next night, Mum left it rather longer before she made Dad visit the parlour, and again he made no comment. The third night he went unprompted after waiting two hours, and then there was a commotion, the sound of a youth being thrown out, and a girl crying. Mum wanted an explanation. . . .

"Well," said Dad, "I said nothing about him stripping our Mary, I said nothing when I found him doing our Mary, that's what they call 'progress' I thought, but I do draw the line when I find him wiping his filthy wick on our best curtains."

ALL BALLS

An old couple had promised themselves a seaside holiday when the husband retired. Foolishly, they did not book, and every hotel in Seaville was full. Worn out, they went to the Police Station, where a kind Inspector took pity. "There's just one manager who'll fix you up as a favour to me," he said, "take this note to the Majestic."

The manager said that as a favour he would open up the bridal suite, but the old man was not grateful:

"Her and me's 65, what would we want with a bridal suite!" The annoyed manager said: "Look you old sod, I've slept people in the billiard room before now, but they didn't have to play billiards all night!"

CLOSED SHOP

One day old Maggie asked her husband, as they were going to bed, what would become of them when he could no longer work. Old Jack said: "Look out of the window, I own those two cottages, and the shop on the corner."

The wife wanted to know how he had done this on a modest wage. . . .

"From the day we were wed, I put a half-crown under the mattress every time you let me."

"Well I never!"

"Yes, and if you hadn't been such a cold mean frigid old sod we'd have had two hotels and a pub!"

IN AND OUT THE WINDOW'S

Two men were on a walking tour of the New Forest when they got caught in a black storm and lost their way. After wandering around until dark they became very tired, but happened to see a light in the distance. Struggling across, they found it was the abode of a presentable widow, who made them welcome with supper and wine.

As the evening drew to a close she said: "You are both decent respectable looking men, so I suggest that you toss up; the loser sleeps in the spare room, the winner sleeps with me."

Jack won the toss, and had a marvellous night of it.

Next morning, well fortified with breakfast, they set off in bright sunshine to resume their travels. There was a long pregnant silence before Bill said:

"How d'yer get on?"

"Marvellous! but in the morning she began to get worried, and pressed for my name and address, so I gave her yours."

This led to a bitter quarrel, and the break-up of the friendship, until some nine months later Bill called on Jack:

"Hey," he said, "you remember that widow? Well, I've had a solicitor's letter and . . ."

"Look," said Jack, "I'm very sorry, old pal, I know I let you down, but what could I do, you know what my wife is, she'd have . . ."

"I was saying," said Bill icily, "before you interrupted me, I was saying, she's died and left me five thousand pounds."

THE ELASTIC LIMIT

A boy of twelve was sent to the psychologist because he was such a complete pest. He made catapults all the time, and broke everything in sight.

The Head Shrinker was convinced that "sex" lay behind everything, and he asked the kid what he would do if he found himself alone for the afternoon in the house with a girl his own age.

"I'd kiss and fondle her to get her in a nice mood."

(Here we go, thought the psychologist).

"What next?"

"I'd get her in the mood and take her knickers off."

"What would you do after that?"

"Next," said the kid "I'd get out my pocket knife and threaten her with it to make her give way to my wishes."

"Which would be what . . .?"

"Why mister, I'd want to cut her knickers up to get the elastic out and make some more catapults."

THEN THE BALLOON WENT UP

A small boy wandered into his mother's bathroom when she forgot to lock the door, and said:

"Mother, what nice balloons you've got!"

"Balloons, Jimmy, why do you call them balloons?"

"Well, I saw father blowing the maid's up when you were out yesterday."

HOLY LIFE

There was a man who lived a righteous and upright life, while his neighbour loved drinking and fornicating, which were his two main hobbies.

In course of time the wicked man died as the result of his excesses, whilst still a young man, and the good respectable neighbour continued to flourish, and be a pillar of the church.

At last, however, the second man died, and, naturally, went straight to Heaven. Imagine his surprise however, when he got inside, to see his old neighbour apparently doing more than well. The wicked man was sitting at the side of a large barrel of beer, and in his arms was a naked lady angel with obvious and luscious attractions.

The pillar of the church hastened off to Saint Peter and complained bitterly:

"Look," he said, "I denied myself all the good things of life, on earth, so that I could come to Heaven, and have the consolation of knowing that Smith was in hell; now look at him . . . unlimited beer and a naked girl to. . . ."

"Stop!" said Saint Peter, "the man is in hell, as he deserves to be."

"In hell?" said the other, "in hell? I can't say that's my idea of hell!"

"Ah," said Peter, "that's because you don't know the facts."

"What facts?"

"Well, you see, the barrel's got a hole in it, but the woman hasn't."

FEATHERBEDDED

A man was crossing a wild heath late on a filthy night, when his car broke down. He staggered on for some miles, and at last came to a lonely cottage, where an old couple were just going to bed. The old man looked at the wet and shivering stranger and said:

"We've only got two bedrooms and our spinster daughter sleeps in the other one, but you can lie downstairs on the sofa.

The chap was well pleased, but such a bitter wind got up in the night that Mother woke Father and said:

"Go down and see how he is."

So Father went down to the unhappy stranger and said:

"We're poor folk, but seeing it's so cold, would you like our eiderdown?"

"Good lord no! She's been down twice already."

STORY WITH WHISKERS ON

It was a family re-union, and everybody had to double up. Young Willy, who was 13, and of an enquiring turn of mind, was put to sleep with a young and attractive "Auntie".

No sooner was the light out, than Willy's hands began to wander. Auntie wriggled about to avoid his clutch, and bade him behave himself.

Finally his hand went under her armpit, and he said:

"Oh, you crafty madam, you've shifted it."

THE BLIND

There was a couple went on honeymoon and retired to bed early, in their hired bungalow.

It was late when they finally got up, the sun shining outside.

"Charles, get out of bed please, and let the blind up, I haven't got the strength," said the bride.

Charles got out of bed to do as he was asked, but when the blind went up, he went up with it!

When he had somewhat recovered, the man opened the window, and said to a passing policeman: "Excuse me officer, what time do the Sunday papers arrive around here?"

"Sunday papers!" said the policeman, "today's Wednesday."

NO FLIES ON HIM

There was a spinster sitting knitting in the corner of a railway carriage on a long journey. The only other person in the carriage was a student type who lolled back in the opposite corner.

The old maid observed that the young man's flies were undone. He didn't seem to know or care, and began to doze off. The rolling of the train was producing an effect which made bad worse, and the spinster was getting very concerned. Finally she reached over, nudged him, and said:

"Excuse me young man, excuse me."

"Yes, what is it, Miss?"

"Well, er, well, it really is very wicked of you, but you've got your thing sticking out."

"Miss, you flatter yourself, it's hanging out."

PUTTING ONE AND ONE TOGETHER

There was a couple got married, and the reception was at her home. Half way through the reception, Father called for order, and said: "The bride will now cut the cake."

At this there was confusion, the bride and groom had disappeared!

"Hey mother, where's John and Mary?" roared father.

"Don't panic and take on so, Father," said mother, "they've only gone upstairs a minute, to put their things together."

FROLICS

There was a couple on honeymoon who went to bed in an expensive hotel. Having had a very tiring day, and then having exhausted themselves in the jousts of Venus, the couple tried to go to sleep. However, there was a great deal of noise coming from downstairs, and the longer they lay there trying to doze off, the more the noise increased. Finally the groom rang the bell for the night porter. . . .

"What the hell's going on in this place?" he roared.

"Sorry, Sir, but they're holding the Oddfellow's Ball."

"Oh, are they, well for cripes sake tell them to let go of it."

COCKSURE

A mother was dressing her daughter for the wedding. "Darling, aren't you the weeniest bit nervous?" enquired Momma.

"Certainly not mother! I was never so cocksure in my life."

Titian was mixing rose madder
To paint a lewd nude on a ladder
The condition of Titian,
Indicated coition
So he rushed up the ladder and 'ad 'er!

There was a young lady of Hitchin
Who was scratching her quim in the kitchen
Her mother said: "Rose
"It's the pox I suppose?"
She snapped: "Rollocks get on with your stitchin'."

There once was a spinster named Perkins
Whose gardener gave her some gherkins,
And times out of number
She tried his cucumber
Which swelled up her internal workings.

There was a young Scottie named Coates
Who wearied of living on groats,
For a change, in the end
He married a Friend
And nightly enjoys Quaker oats!

There was a young lady named Hyde
Who tried a banana and cried
And stormed, and lamented
That the fruit had fermented
Inside her, inside her inside

You have to stand on a chair

A very wealthy spinster rang the Grande Hotel to book a suite. The Manager laid on everything of the best, but no sooner were her trunks carried up than she sent for him, and said:

"This is a *dreadful* room! I look out of the window across the courtyard, and what do I see but men undressing, and running about naked."

The Manager leapt to the window, and he looked right and he looked left, but no naked men could he see. . . .

"What men do you refer to, Madam? I can't see any."

"Oh, well of course, you have to stand on a chair."

DEAD EASY

A certain prominent business man lost his wife, and the funeral became a public occasion. All the dignitaries of the town attended, and almost all were known to the bereaved. There was however a stranger, and he seemed more upset than anyone, and before the funeral was over he broke down completely.

The widower-husband asked who was this weeping stranger. . . .

"Ooh!" whispered someone, "didn't you know? He was your late wife's lover!"

The bereaved moved across to the sobbing man, patted him on the back, and said:

"Cheer up old boy, cheer up, I shall probably marry again."

GETTING THE MESSAGE THROUGH

A man went up to the West End looking for tarts. To each girl in turn he said: "Have you got the pox?" and when each indignantly said "No" he turned and walked away.

Finally one girl said: "In all London I only know one girl on the game who's got a dose. . . ."

"Take me to her," said the man, "and I'll pay her double, and give you a present as well."

"Listen, chap, are you barmy, or what?"

"I'll explain: If I can catch the pox I can go home and give it the maid, who'll give it my father, who'll give it my mother, who'll give it the vicar, who'll give it his daughter; she'll give it to her headmaster, and that's the old devil I'm after."

CHIPS OFF THE OLD JOCK?

There was a mean old Scot who suddenly surprised his three sons by saying he would buy them each a present, provided it was something tartan.

"I want a tartan bonnet," cried the first, quickly.

"I want a tartan kilt," cried the second, more bold.

"I want fifty pounds," said the youngest.

"Fifty pounds!! what are you thinking o' getting?"

"I'm not, father, I've got it already!"

"Got what?"

"I've got a tart 'n trouble!"

ALL FOR LOVE

Three sisters fell on hard times when their factory closed
down. When they were very hungry and behind with the
rent, they held a council, and decided that one of them
would have to go on the streets. The first said she was too
old, the second said she was too plain, and it came down to
the youngest to go out and find a customer. For all she
protested her virtue they removed her knickers and left her
standing outside a pub. She was instructed to ask for at least
£3.

It was very late when she got in. "Hurry up!" they said,
"before the fish and chip shop shuts."

"I haven't got any money!"

"Why, what happened?"

The young sister explained that a man had picked her up,
taken her to a room, stripped her bare, had his will twice,
and given her three pounds. . . .

"Come on then, what did you do with it?"

"Well, you see, I liked it so much, I gave it him back to
do it again."

BUS OR PRAM?

Two women, strangers had been waiting at the bus stop for
ages. Finally one spoke:

"When's it due?"

"March!"

"Cripes, the ruddy service gets worse don't it."

CHEAP AT HALF THE PRICE

An Alderman had to go to London, and his wife tagged along. While he was at the Ministry she went shopping, and they arranged to meet for tea. The Alderman's business being soon finished, he went looking for a tart. In the West End he met a Real High Class, and it was all arranged when the girl mentioned that it would be ten pounds.

"Struth! I've only got thirty shillings."

So she left him flat, and the man collected his wife and took her to a restaurant. At the next table sat the "model" he had picked up an hour before. She leaned over and said very loudly:

"Serves you right, that's what you get for thirty shillings."

LOVE FROM A STRANGER

A man swore that if his Premium Bond came up, he'd do a good deed. He won a good prize, so he told the Warden of an Old Peoples Home to choose a deserving couple and he would send them to Blackpool for a weekend.

"No, you go in and pick your own."

The man picked his couple, gave them money, vouchers and everything needed for a luxury hotel visit. After they were back the donor met the woman one day in the street. She thanked him very much, and went on. . . .

"By the way, who was that gay old kipper you sent with me?"

A BLOCK OFF THE OLD CHIPPY

A frustrated spinster was a pest to the police, she kept ringing up saying there was a man under her bed. She was sent to a Mental Hospital, but she still told the doctors there was a man under her bed. They gave her the latest drugs, and she suddenly declared she was cured.

"You mean, Miss Rustyfan, you can't see a man under the bed now?"

"No I can't. I can see two."

One doctor told the other that there was only really one sort of injection that would cure her complaint, which he called "Malignant virginity" – why did they not shut her up in her bedroom with Big Dan, the hospital carpenter?

Big Dan was fetched, told what her complaint was, and told he would be locked in with her for an hour. He said it wouldn't take that long, and an anxious group gathered on the landing . . . they heard:

"No, stop it, Dan, mother would never forgive."

"Shut up yelling, it's got to be done some time, it should have been done years ago."

"Have your way by force then, you brute!"

"It's only what your husband would have done, had you had one."

The medics could not wait, they burst in.

"I've cured her," said the carpenter.

"He's cured me," said Miss Rustyfan.

He had sawn the legs off the bed.

BOARD AND LODGINGS

The old Pioneer and the young Pioneer were off on the Yukon trail. They slogged on and on, pulling a sledge, until they came to the last outpost, which was simply a place in the snow where two tracks crossed, and there was a hutted store.

The old Pioneer entered the Store and said:

"Howde, pard – got my gunpowder?"

"Yes, Jake."

"Got my traps, got my pemmican?"

"Yes, sure thing, here y'are."

"Got my board all ready?"

"Yep, all wrapped up and ready."

* * *

So they loaded stores and resumed their treck. Soon the young Pioneer said: "Hey, what's this about a board, what the heck do we wanna board for?"

The old Pioneer explained that in the Yukon it was possible to go six months without seeing a woman, therefore the old and experienced traveller arranged to have a board with a hole in it, and a naked woman painted on it.

* * *

Only a short time later Jake returned to the Store, alone.

"Gees, Jake, youze back early, didya strike gold or what?"

"Nope, just a bit o' bad luck I had, had to shoot me pardner."

"Hadta shoot yer pardner, that's bad. For Pete's sake, why?"

"Caught that guy sleeping with ma board."

FOR BEDDER OR WORSE

A Cambridge student rushed into his friend's study unannounced. His friend was not there, so he went on into the bedroom, and there was his friend lying face down on the bed, on top of a life-size cinema poster.

"I say Charles, old boy, what the bloody h—"

His friend looked up rather breathless and panted:

"It's all right, Mortiboys, I've got the charwoman underneath."

HOLE IN NONE

Four middle-aged men were on a Irish golf course. The little quiet feller was just teeing off when a leprechaun appeared to him, and asked if he would like to hole in one.

"Where's the catch in it?"

"Not a catch. You have to give up five years of your sex life, but think of the glory."

The man thought of that, agreed, and holed in one, to the astonishment of the onlookers.

At the next hole, the leprechaun offered another hole-in-one in exchange for ten years of the man's lovelife. The result was sensational, it had only been done four times in history.

The fairy said: "Bet all you've got you can do it three times, the odds will be fantastic, but no relations with any women for the rest of your life, remember!"

And that is how Father O'Flynn got his name in all the record books.

A TRIPLE EVENT

A father approached his child of ten and said: "I think I'd better tell you, your mother's going to have another baby; it's in her tummy now, waiting to be born."

"Are you sure, daddy?"

"Of course I'm sure, what are you looking so worried about?"

"Well, daddy, auntie says the stork's bringing me a brother or a sister, and will drop it down the bedroom chimney; Mrs Smith says the doctor will be bringing one in a little black bag, so it looks as if the bloody place'll soon be overrun with kids."

THE PRIMROSE PATH

There was a mother of two boys who said to her oldest: "Look you're eighteen now, your father's dead, I think you should tell your younger brother the facts of life."

The youth sought out his kid brother of sixteen, and said: "Here you, listen, what did we do last night?"

"Why, we went up the boozer, had a couple, and picked up Poppy Tinne and Lucy Tupper the bar-room floozies."

"Yes, go on."

"Well, we bought them some gins, and then we gave them five bob each and took them round the back of the boozer."

"Yes, what next?"

"Well, we took one each, pushed them up against the wall and . . . look, what's all this in aid of?"

"Nothing. It's just that mother says I've got to tell you it's just the same with birds and the bees and the flowers."

NO USA ANY MORE

In the village was an old widower of 80, whose family had long since grown up. He suddenly married a girl of 20, and shortly afterwards astonished the vicar with:

"I shall want you soon parson, there be a christening on the way."

When the vicar had recovered he managed to stammer:

"Congratulations you old rascal; a child eh? Your wife's young yet; is this the first of several?"

"Nay, vicar, no more after this. You see, my big son's left for Americky."

At this a black thought entered the vicar's mind, but he put it away, and said: "I don't follow you Dad, what's your son going to America got to do with it?

"Well, you see, vicar, he used to lift me on and off."

FISHY

A certain youth had a party piece in which he could insert two fingers in his mouth and give a whistle audible a quarter of a mile away.

This man started courting, and one evening he took his girl right out into the countryside. They dallied long, and, as they approached the terminus, the last bus was moving off.

"Stop him – whistle!" cried the girl.

The man put his two fingers to his mouth, paused, and said: "It's a lovely evening, the walk won't hurt us."

PREGNANT WITH POSSIBILITIES

There was an old man in the village who had been a widower many years; he was known to have money. He went to the doctor and asked for a check over. The doctor said, "For a man of 87 you're doing well, why a check up?" The old rascal explained that he was going to marry a girl of twenty.

He would not be dissuaded, so the doctor's final advice was: "Then, if you hope for a peaceful, not to say a fruitful marriage, take a lodger in as well."

They did not meet for eight months, when the old man said: "Congratulate me doctor, the wife's pregnant."

The doctor collected his thoughts, and said: "Ah yes yes, so you took my advice, and had a lodger as well?"

"Of course, grinned the old devil through his toothless gums, she's pregnant as well!"

THREE TIMES A DAY AFTER MEALS

A courting couple went into a chemists shop, and after some shy whispering the girl said:

"What's that stuff they advertise – 'Makes bonny babies'?"

"Ah," said the pharmacist, "you mean Glaxo, do you want a medium or a large size?"

"Just a minute," said the girl, "who has to take it, me, or my young man?"

FUN WITH DUCKS

A young man married and took his girl to one of these farms where they did holiday accommodation, for their honeymoon.

Half way through the week, over breakfast, the farmer hummed and ha'd a bit and then said:

"Look here, are you two getting enough?"

"I don't know what you mean!" stammered the man.

"I mean, enough to eat?"

"Oh, yes, plenty thanks, why?"

"I only thought," said the farmer, "that if you must keep eating sausages in the bedroom, I wish you wouldn't throw the skins out of the window, they be choking my ducks."

STRETCHING IT A BIT

A man consulted his doctor because his wife was having far too many children. The doctor gave him a sheath and said follow the instructions and all would be well.

A month later the man was back saying his wife was pregnant again. . . .

"Did you follow the instructions?"

"Well doctor, it said: 'Stretch over the organ before intercourse', but as we hadn't got an organ I stretched it over the piano. . . ."

JUST A PRECAUTION

Twins were waiting to be born; said one:

"Don't let's go out yet."

Said the other: "Why not?"

"It's raining outside."

"How d'you know?"

"There's a man just come up the entry with his mac on!"

GETTING HIS MEMBER IN

A Socialist girl and a Tory man were very much in love, and finally married. On the first night of their wedding, instead of love and passion, they finished up in a double bed with their backs turned on each other, all because of a silly quarrel about politics.

After twenty minutes a timid girl's voice said:

"Darling."

"Yes, what is it?"

"There's a split in the Labour Party, and if the Conservative member stood now, he'd get in easily."

"Too bloody late! He's stood as an independent, and lost his deposit."

ICE-HOLES TO YOU

A hunter tried to catch a polar bear for a zoo, but had no luck, until an Eskimo, in exchange for whisky, told him what to do . . .

"They love dried peas. You make a neat hole in the ice, three feet across, and each night you put dried peas round the edge. After a few days he gets over-confident, then, you creep up behind him quietly and . . ."

"And what?"

"Kick him in the ice-hole!"

MISTAKEN IDENTITY

The husband gets drunk, and insists on taking a friend home from pub to show him posh home. They get in the hall, and:

"Shee that chandelier, thash mine!"

They progress through the house. . . . "Shee that gran' pianer, thash mine."

"Shee that colour tel'vision shet, thash mine."

Then upstairs: "Shee that king-shise double bed, thash mine."

"Shee that lovely woman naked in bed, thash my wife."

"Shee that feller lyin' on top of her. Thash me."

DO OR DIE

Dai was popular in the Welsh village, and easily won at the Rural District Election. "Congratulations Dai!" said the barman in the local.

"Councillor Jones, now, if you please."

The landlord came in – "Congratulations Dai!"

"Councillor Jones from now, IF you don't mind."

The Minister popped in for a lemonade – "Well done Dai!"

"Councillor Jones now, Minister, please."

He went home late and rather sloshed, and the house was dark but for a light upstairs. As he entered, a voice from above said:

"Is that you, Dai?"

"Shertainly not!" was the very slurred response, "Ish Counshellor Jones."

"Oh good, but come on up quick, we've only got a few minutes and Dai'll be coming home."

TICKED OFF

A young couple with single beds had been married a month when they realised someone had stolen their alarm clock. They sat down and thought and thought, and working it out backwards, they remembered that on the day of the wedding, Uncle Geroge had been seen much admiring the clock. Taking a chance, they wrote and asked him if by any chance he could say what had happened to it – had he by accident walked off with it?

A telegram came back: "In the other bed you fools."

HARD AND SOFT

A "Modern" couple started off their married life with single beds. One night soon after they had turned in, a little voice was heard:

"Ooh, dahling." – – – – – – "Yes dahling?"

"Would poppa's likkle iggy-wiggy lovvy-duvvy cuddle-some girl like to come over into this ikkle warm beddy?"

She replied: "Of course poppas ikkle sugar-bunch wants to come into dahlin's beddy-weddy," but alas on the way over she tripped on the mat, and he said: "Oh honey, oh likkle dewdrop, diddums hurtums ikkle self?"

But, she had't hurt herself, and was soon locked with him in the jousts of Venus. Fifteen minutes later, when returning to her own bed, she fell over the mat again. . . .

"Why don't you look where you're putting your great big ugly feet you stupid little fool!!!!"

NO TREAD!

A very shapely girl got married to a young man who was mad about motor cars and everything to do with them. After they had been married a week the girl's father happened to meet her, and asked her how she was getting on.

"It's terrible," she said, "he gets into bed and goes straight to sleep, he doesn't *do* anything!"

Father thought for a moment and said: "Listen, when you go to bed tonight, lie flat on your back, and as he begins to doze off, take hold of his hand and stroke it straight down the middle of your belly: nature will do the rest."

The girl carefully remembered her instructions, and when they were in bed, took hold of her sleepy husband's hand and stroked the palm of it down her tummy. Her husband suddenly cried out: "Scandalous, I've been swindled! Only five hundred miles and not a bit of tread left on it."

SHORT TRIPS

A girl was courting a sailor, and he used to send her all his money to get a home together ready for the wedding day. When at last he came home to make her his bride, she showed him with pride the house she had got, and the furniture in it. All went well until he saw the bridal bedroom, in which were twin beds.

"Twin beds, by cripes what's this, a joke?"

"Darling, darling think of the money we shall save."

"Rubbish, think of the carpets we shall wear out!"

EXPENSIVE BOARD!

A man's wife died, and he decided to get right away on a long-distance cargo boat. After a while he began to regret it, and said: "Captain, what do we do for sex?" Said the Captain: "You know damn well Australia is three months away; there's nothing doing."

A week later the man returned to the old subject:

"What do the crew do for sex?"

"I'll tell you, they have a board with a naked female painted on it, and a hole in it; the cook bends down on the other side. I daresay they'll give you a turn if you'll pay."

So the man had a go, and the Captain said:

"That'll be six pounds two and six."

"What?! How can it be that much?."

"Half a crown for the cook, and two pounds each for the men who hold him; you see, he don't like it very much."

BLACK AND WHITE

A negro boy came home painted white, and said:

"The kids at school painted me white all over," so his mother beat him for getting messed up. Father came home, and said: "What's going on?" so Mother told him: "The kids at school painted our Sam white." So father gave him another thrashing for not standing up for himself. Shortly afterwards a small voice was heard:

"I've only been a white boy for two hours but already I hate you black b*ggers."

There was a young fellow of Poole
Who found a red ring round his tool,
He ran to the clinic,
But the doctor, a cynic,
Said: "That's only lipstick, you fool!"

A Magdalen Dean of Divinity
Had a daughter who kept her virginity,
The Fellows of Magdalen
They must have been dawdlin'
'Twould never have happened at Trinity

There was a young fellow of Trinity
Who ruined his sister's virginity
He rogered his brother
Had twins by his mother –
And now he's a Dean of Divinity!

There was a good Bishop of Birmingham
Who did all young girls whilst confirming 'em,
Amidst screams of applause
He dragged off their drawers,
And slipped the episcopal worm in 'em!

Two school-kids around Aberystwyth
Made love with the lips that they kissed with
But as they grew older
They also grew bolder
Making love with the things that they pissed with

Repairs to gun

A man went for a job as a Commercial Traveller, and told the Sales Manager he was the best in the business provided his expenses were met without dispute.

"No bother at all," said the latter, "you sell the stuff, we pay up without question."

In the first few months the man doubled the sales, but sent in a bill for £45. He was told that on those sort of figures he must set out the details.

Accordingly, next time, the bill showed such items as:

Intercourse with Molly	=	£5
Laying Big Mabel	=	£4
Knee-trembler, Mrs Loveit	=	£3
		and so on . . .

The Sales Manager was aghast because these matters were dealt with by young girls in the Accounts Section, and the Traveller was ordered to disguise his goings-on in diplomatic terms. So, month after month there appeared:

"Shooting = £3" or "Game Birds = £10" and so on, and all went well.

However, after a wonderful year the accounts stopped coming in, and so did the orders. The firm wrote anxiously to enquire progress, and received no reply except:

Repairs to gun   =   £150

HOT STUFF

A man got married, and when he returned to work after his honeymoon, all his mates "ribbed" him.

"Come on Jack," said one, "how's your wife now?"

"I left her smoking in bed this morning," he replied.

"Cripes, what lovemaking," said an envious forewoman.

BOOT ON THE OTHER FOOT?

A commercial traveller, staying at a hotel, fancied the chambermaid. He offered her £5 for an hour upstairs, but the girl replied indignantly that she was not like that. She added that when she did it was for love, not money, and just now she had "gone off" and could not get passionate if she tried.

The traveller played his trump card, he was selling shoes, and here was an extremely fine sample pair. . . .

The girl's vanity conquered, and she took the traveller upstairs, stripped naked, and lay back on the bed. The traveller got going, and to his delight found the girl very responsive. She wrapped her right arm round him, then her left leg, then her left arm, then her right leg, and he found these wriggles and embraces delicious.

"I thought you said you couldn't get worked up?"

"I'm not," she replied, "I'm simply trying the shoes on."

FRENCH LEAVE

A Frenchman staying at an English country house for the weekend was attracted to a Debutante type, and without much difficulty, seduced her. Several months later they met by chance at a very select Society ball. He stepped forward with outstretched hand, but she walked straight past him without acknowledgement. As soon as he could, the Frenchman cornered her and said: "Surely you remember me?"

Of course I do young man, but you are not to assume that in England a one-night frolic constitutes an introduction."

EXPOSED HIS WEAKNESS

A well-built navvy was signing on at the "Labour" when when one day the clerk said: "Would you like to have a go at this job? It's a middle-aged spinster lady, very wealthy. Her butler's died, and she must have a big lusty man in the livery, even if he can't buttle."

So off went the navvy to the Great House, again assured by the Labour Exchange that his ignorance was no bar.

He returned, crestfallen.

"How did you get on?"

"I got on lovely at first; she said stand up straight, turn round, yes, yes, try the coat on, and I did perfect. She smiled and said: I'm sure you'll do, now show me your testimonials."

"Believe me mister, I lorst that job through sheer bloody ignorance."

WHO'RE YOU SPEAKING OF?

The small urchins playing in a back street. Rolls Royce arrives, befurred and bejewelled young woman gets out and cries: "Willy!"

The snottier of the two raggamuffins goes over and the girl says: "Here's five pounds, take it straight to mother. Here's five shillings, that's for you, now be a good boy!"

With which she re-entered the chauffeur-driven Phantom, and disappeared in a cloud of perfume.

"Hey, 'oo's that?" said the other kid.

"That's my sister wot's bin ruined."

COLD LOVER

There was a man had a most attractive wife, but he began to be suspicious of her. At last he could stand it no longer. Being on "nights" he asked the foreman for a "pass-out" and went home at two in the morning to find his best friend's car outside, just as he had feared.

He let himself in, crept up the stairs, and rushed into his wife's bedroom. There she lay, on top of the bed, stark naked, but smoking a cigarette and reading a book.

He went wild and searched under the bed, in the wardrobe, even in the airing cupboard, but he could find no man. He went berserk, wrecked the bedroom, then he started on the living room, threw the TV out of the window, slashed the armchairs, overturned the table and sideboard, then turned his attention to the kitchen, where he smashed all the crocks and threw the fridge out of the window. Then he shot himself.

When he got up to Heaven's gates, who should he see waiting for admission, but his late best friend, who said:

"What are you doing up here?"

So the wronged husband explained how he had lost his temper, and all about it, and added: "But how does it come about that you are up here too?"

"Oh me? I was in the fridge."

A FUNNEL FOR THE MISSUS

There was an old farmer who all his life had wanted to stay at an expensive hotel. At last he achieved his aim, but, as he and the old woman went to bed, he observed something lacking. He asked the night porter, where was the chamber pot?

The man explained that they didn't have them, but there was a bathroom at the end of the corridor. The farmer said he didn't want a bath, and the end of the matter was, the night porter, in exchange for half a crown, fetched an empty quart bottle.

"Well Sir, how did you get on?" he enquired next morning.

"I was all right," said the old farmer, "myself, but I was up half the night trying to make a funnel for the missus."

HE FLUSHED

A man who had been living in the slums was granted a council house.

"How's it going?" asked a mate at work, a few days later. Jack explained that it was a bit of all right, except for that mysterious chain and tank arrangement in the bathroom.

"Why! You bloody fool, you pull down the chain, and that makes the water flow."

The next day, Jack said he'd tried it out, but it was no good.

"What went wrong?"

"Well, I pulled the chain, and the water came, like you said, but before I could grab the soap and towel, it had all gone again."

THE RESULT OF PRAYER

Two girl friends married on the same day, and took their new husbands to the same honeymoon hotel. The four of them sat in the lounge thinking how obvious it would look if they all went to bed at the same early hour, but after a while it was decided that the girls should go out in the direction of the "Ladies" and then slip up to their rooms, and the men would have a last drink at the bar. After about ten or fifteen minutes the men would leave casually in the same manner, and join their brides.

However, just as they were about to follow the girls, every light in the place failed, which was disconcerting in a strange building. Nevertheless, each was convinced he could find his room, and so they set off.

Harry groped up stairs and along passages, counting doors in his careful way (for he was a very careful man) and found the room. Just to make sure he struck a match and saw bits of confetti on the landing. Then, quietly entering he carefully took off his clothes, put on his pyjamas, kneeled down and said his prayers, climbed into bed, and began to make love.

At that very moment all the lights came on, and he saw that he was in the "right room" as it were, but on the wrong floor, and this was the other man's bride! He grabbed his clothes and hurried off to his own proper room, only to find that the other man was an atheist!

OPENED HER MONEY BOX

Two business girls shared a flat. One night one of them was out on a date, and her friend went to bed. She had not been in bed long when the other one returned, and, not wishing to disturb her mate, got undressed in the dark. As she did so, there was a curious tinkling noise. As neither of them could make sense of this, they went to sleep.

In the morning Jane said: "Hey Mary, what was that rattling last night when you were going to bed?"

"I don't know Jane, let's look round."

They scrabbled on the floor, and found an American dime.

"Oh the swine!" said Mary, "he told me it would melt in three minutes."

PERIODS

Two friends got married about the same time. After five years Pat, the Roman Catholic had one child, Jack, the Protestant, had four. One Saturday they were drinking, and Jack asked Pat how it was that he, an RC had fathered only one child, while he Jack, was fathering one a year.

"It's the 'safe period'," said Pat.

"Garn! The doctors say it doesn't work."

"It works if you know exactly when it is, it's different for each individual. In my case, I have sex every third week, late at night, weekdays only."

"Well Pat, why is that the safe period for you?"

"You see Jack, that's when you're on nights."

A certain fishing club ran an annual outing. One year, when they were preparing the outing, the Chairman said:

"Look, just for once we'd better take the ladies; my wife is for ever on at me that we clear off fishing every weekend, and we never take them anywhere."

After discussions this was agreed on, and the day of the outing came round. It turned out to be nothing but a long booze-up, and only after the last pub' was closed did they make for home. It was a long way, and after a while the Chairman told the driver he must make a comfort stop.

"Impossible!" said the driver, "this is a 'No stopping highway'."

The coach went on and on and on, and the men were bursting. Finally the Chairman said: "Never mind the law, stop soon for cripes sake."

"O.K.," said the driver, "if you're that desperate I'll stay in the next lay-by, but it's got a street lamp in it, you'll have to put up with that.'

He stopped by the lamp, while drunk and desperate men got out and relieved themselves, neither knowing nor caring what the wives, sitting in the bus, could see.

Late that night, going to bed, the Chairman's wife said:

"You are nothing but a lot of disgusting beasts. First you get stupid drunk, then you flash yourselves without shame in front of a whole bus full of wives . . ." she stopped for breath, and then continued:

"Mind you Jack, I was very proud of ours!"

BISHOP'S BAD BACK

Three Business men were off to a conference. They sat in the train with a parson. One buried his head in the Times, the other two conversed – What will you do with your spare time at Brighton? asked the first. Replied the second: Pubs! they've got wonderful pubs there, not one will remain unvisited – what will you do?

Girls! replied the other. Brighton's full of girls, all sorts of girls, I'm off on the tiles every night!

The parson was shocked, and was about to make some remark when the Delegate who was reading the Times looked up, and said: Does anybody know what sciatica is?

Yes! said the parson quickly, it is a painful disease caused by alcoholic indulgence, and promiscuity.

Ah, that's very odd, said the questioner, for I see that your Bishop has got a bad attack of it!

TAKING A CHANCE

There was a fireman who was horribly mean both to his wife and his lodger. One night he brought home a splendid pork pie and ate half of it for his supper. His wife and the lodger had to make do with dry bread and cheese.

He carefully put the rest of the pie away, and they all went to their beds.

In the middle of the night the fire bells rang, and off the landlord had to run. The wife, stark naked, entered the lodger's room, shook him awake and said: "He's gone out, quick, now's your chance."

"Are you sure it's all right?" enquired the lodger

"Of course! Hurry up, lose no time!"

So the lodger went downstairs and finished the pork pie.

LOOK LIVELY!

A chap went to bed with his wife, and he was just dozing off when she shook him hard. . . .

"John, don't go to sleep darling! Listen, I've made a mistake and instead of my sleeping tablets I've taken my pep pills. . . ."

"Aha! Whacko!, and you want me to . . . ?"

"Yes, of course, I want you to teach me the Gay Gordons."

DOWN WITH THE PILL

Two farmers drinking, and one says to the other:

"How is it your stock breed so well, and mine are hardly breeding at all?"

The other explained that he was getting some special sex-pills from the Vet to give the animals.

"Sex pills, what be they? What's in them?"

"Oh, I don't know what's in 'em, but they taste like peppermints."

BAG AND BAGGAGE

A man was going to a distant town on business, and not taking his wife. He asked his pal if he'd got any addresses. His pal said; "any house in Blanco Street will produce women who've got everything a man could wish for."

The stranger knocked on many doors, and each produced a slut more odious than the last. He had nearly given up hope, when, at the last house the door was answered by a woman with everything a man might wish for . . . beard, moustache, muscles. . . .

THE BOSS, THE TYPIST, AND THE LINGERIE

On the staff of Beatherfed UDC was a young woman of excellent figure who was considered "fast". She was, however, popular with her male colleagues, all of whom claimed at some time or other to have had her favours. All, that is, except the Head Clerk, who was oldish, and somewhat crabby. He dropped her several hints, but all in vain.

Suddenly, last year just before Christmas, she said to him: "It's my birthday to-morrow – I thought perhaps you'd like to come down in the evening, bring a bottle of wine and cut yourself a slice of cake."

Overjoyed, he arrived on time, bottles bulging from his pockets, and knocked the outer door. She admitted him to the lobby, and said: "Wait a minute darling, I'm not quite ready," with which she disappeared within. He waited about fifteen minutes, and was getting properly cheesed off, when the inner door opened, and she stood there in ravishing black nylon lingerie.

I'll not keep you long now," she said, "I'm nearly ready – why don't you strip off while you're waiting."

Sure enough, in a few minutes a sweet voice called: "Coo-ee, come i-in darli-i-ing."

He needed no second bidding! He stepped boldly in, his clothes (neatly folded) over his left arm, his shoes held in his right hand. There she sat, lit by soft candles, more desirable than ever. Her table was loaded with food and wine. Round it, in festive attire, sat fourteen men and women – the whole office staff – wearing paper hats.

A HAND IN THINGS

A mother and her seventeen-year-old daughter sat on a bus. Outside the hospital a man got on who had been in an accident, and he had both his arms in slings.

When the conductor came round for the money the man said:

"Excuse me Miss, will you put your hand in my trousers pocket and get out a shilling for my fare."

The girl did this, but she was so embarrassed that she dropped the money, and it rolled under the seats, causing quite a kerfuffle.

When they got off the bus, the woman said:

"Really Mary, you did make a lot of fuss and bother over nothing, you could see the poor man could not help himself, and yet you go all goofy, just over putting your hand in his pocket."

She said: "Oh mother, I did feel a big soft thing."

A PILL IN THE EAR

"Oh yes," said this working-class woman. "Nye Bevan was the greatest man wno ever lived."

"Why's that Mrs Moggs?"

"Well luv, he started this here National Health and saved me from having about fourteen kids."

"But don't be silly Mrs Moggs, you don't get birth control on the National Health!"

"Course yer do, I get me deaf aid on it. Saved me having a string o' kids it did."

"I don't foller yer Mrs Moggs, how could a deaf aid stop yer having kids?"

"I'll tell yer, Mrs Bloggs: every night when we went to bed me and my old man, he'd say: 'Are we going to go to sleep or what?' and me being so deaf I'd say 'what'.

PUT HIS FOOT IN IT

A man stayed out late, drinking, and crept into bed in the dark. When he awoke at daybreak he saw three pairs of feet sticking out at the bottom of the bed, and one was a black pair. He woke his wife up, and said:

"Hey Mary, look at that, three pairs!"

She said: "Don't talk bloody daft, you're drinking yourself stupid, go down and count them." So the husband got out, carefully counted and examined the objects, and said:

"You're quite right, only two pairs, and aint mine dirty!"

IT'S THE KNACK AS DOES IT

A young bull, newly on the farm, was put in with the old bull.

"What would you like to do?" enquired the old bull.

"Well, I hear there's a hundred cows right across the far side of the farm; I suggest we run over and do two or three each?"

"Certainly not! We'll WALK there, and do them all."

SQUATTERS RIGHTS

An Indian Chief came into big money when oil was discovered on his reservation, so he booked a room in a London hotel for himself and his favourite squaw. In the night he woke her up with:

"Big Chief, him want water, plenty water."

She fetched him some, but from then on, about every hour he made the same demand. Finally he got a refusal:

"Big Chief, him no can have water! White woman sitting on well."

LOST AND FOUND

"Is that the Salvation Army?"
   "Yes, speaking."
   "Do you save lost girls?"
   "Indeed we do!"
   "Save one for Saturday night for me, will you please?"

MAIDEN'S DREAM

A "difficult" schoolgirl of fifteen was sent to the Psychologist, who asked her a number of very personal questions. He was sure that "sex" lay at the bottom of the trouble, and asked her:
   "Do you suffer from sexy or erotic dreams?"
   "Certainly not!"
   "Are you sure?"
   "Quite sure, in fact, I enjoy them."

IN A JAM

Two strawberries were cooking in a pot, and it got hotter and more uncomfortable every moment. Said one to the other:
   "You know, if us two hadn't been found in the same bed, we wouldn't be in this jam now."

SHOWED HER PINK FORM

A working girl who applied for a job at a big factory was told to fill in the usual form calling for name, address, age, etc., etc.
   She brought it back and under the heading "Sex" had entered: "Four times a week."

WHAT THE BUTLER DIDN'T SEE

The London fog was swirling over the Thames as a young tramp settled himself on the embankment for the night.

Suddenly he was roused by a gentle voice and, looking up, saw a beautiful brunette alighting from her chauffeur-driven Rolls-Royce.

"My poor man," she said, "you must be terribly cold and wet. Let me drive you to my home and put you up for the night."

Of course, the tramp didn't refuse this invitation and climbed into the car beside her.

After a short drive the car stopped before a large Victorian mansion and the brunette stepped out, beckoning the tramp to follow her. The door was opened by the butler, into whose charge the lady gave the tramp, with instructions that he should be given a meal, a bath and a comfortable bed in the servants' quarters.

Some while later, as the brunette was preparing to retire, it occurred to her that her guest might be in need of something, so, slipping on her negligee, she hurried along to the servants' wing.

As she rounded the corner a chink of light met her eye, indicating that the young man was awake.

Knocking softly on the door she entered the room and enquired of the young man why he was not sleeping.

"Surely you are not hungry?"

"Oh no, your butler fed me royally."

"Then perhaps your bed is not comfortable?"

"But it is – soft and warm."

"Then you must need company. Move over a little. . . ."
The young man, overjoyed, moved over. . . .

(and fell into the Thames. . . .)

There was a young girl of Madrid
Who wouldn't be done for a quid,
There came an Italian
With a stalk like a stallion
Who swore that he would, and he did!
Now, this clever young girl of Madrid
When she found she was having a kid,
She stopped up her water
For a month and a quarter,
And drownéd the b*gger, she did!

There was a young lady of Durbar
Who swore that no man could curb 'er,
But a man from Khartoum
Knocked the top off her womb
With a fifteen inch kidney disturber!

There was a young lady of Tottenham
Her manners? She'd simply forgotten 'em,
During tea at the Vicar's
She whipped off her knickers,
Because she was feeling too hot in 'em!

There was a young lady of Twickenham
Of candles she never grew sick on 'em,
She prayed in the nude
And Venus she sued –
To-lengthen, and strengthen, and thicken 'em

A Tribute to Mr. Wilson

Dear Secretary – We have the honour to be members of a Committee set up to raise £50,000 for the purpose of erecting a statue to H. Wilson Esq. at Westminster. The Committee is in somewhat of a quandary as to where to place it, it could not go next to that of George Washington who never told a lie, nor Lloyd George who never told the truth, since Harold Wilson could not tell the difference.

After careful consideration we have decided to put it next to Christopher Columbus, the greatest Socialist of them all, in that he started out not knowing where he was going, arriving did not know where he was, and returning, did not know where he had been, and he did all this on borrowed money. The inscription will read: "Five thousand years ago, Moses said to the Children of Israel, 'Pick up your shovels, mount your asses and camels, and I will lead you to the Promised Land'." Nearly 5,000 years later, George Brown said: "Lay down your shovels, sit on your asses, light up a camel, this IS the promised land." Now Wilson is stealing your shovels, kicking your asses, increasing the tax on camels, and taking over the Promised Land.

Therefore, naturally, we expect a generous contribution from you towards our noble project.

Yours,

Wm Muggins

THE DIRECTOR'S LARK

A meeting of the Education Committee was recently called for the purpose of presenting Miss Lark, the Director's Secretary with a testimonial on the occasion of her leaving to take up another sphere of labour.

In making the presentation the Director, Dr Heluva B. Lyar, in a few well-chosen words, referred to Miss Lark's extraordinary capabilities. The Dr remarked that for quickness of conception, easy delivery, and faithful reproduction of all matters imparted to her, Miss Lark surpassed any secretary he had ever had under him, and which, the Director facetiously remarked, had not been few He further remarked that he had never known his efforts with Miss Lark to miscarry.

Miss Lark, in thanking the Director for his great kindness, felt bound to refer to his gentleness, firmness and strength in his treatment of her when she had the pleasure of working under him. Miss Lark spoke feelingly of his energy and force of action, his powers of duration, his dexterity in grasping his subjects, and above all, his precision in driving home his point. Concluding, Miss Lark trusted that the germ so skilfully imparted to her by Dr Heluva B. Lyar would fructify, and if, as she hoped, the Doctor would find time to visit her in her new home, he would find that his labours had not been in vain.

LOVE LETTER

To –

My Dear Ever-Loving Wife

During the past year I have tried to make love to you 365 times, an average of once per day, and the following is a list of the reasons you gave for rejecting me:

Wrong week	11
It will wake the children	7
It is too hot	15
It is too cold	3
Too tired	19
Too late	16
Too early	9
Pretending to sleep	33
Window is open, neighbours might hear	3
Backache	16
Toothache	2
Headache	6
Not in the mood	31
Baby restless, might cry	18
Watched late show	15
Mud-pack	8
Grease on face	4
Too drunk	7
Forgot to visit chemists	10
Visitors sleeping in next room	7
Just had hair done	28
Is that all you think about?	62

Dearest, do you think we can improve on our record during the forthcoming year?

Your ever-loving Husband,

Jack.

THE LADY AND THE LAW

Late one evening two gentlemen were walking down the avenue when they passed a very respectable-looking girl. As she passed one says to the other: "I'd give fifty pounds to spend a night with her." The girl overheard, turned, and said: "It's a bargain"! The man immediately said Goodnight to his friend and took the lady to her flat.

The next morning the man got up, put £25 on the dresser, and prepared to go. She asked for the rest of the money, adding "If you don't pay up I'll sue you for it." The man laughed, and departed.

A few days later, he got a Summons. He rushed off to his Solicitor, who said: "She can't possibly recover from you for *that*, but it will be interesting to see what her lawyer makes of it.

After the usual preliminaries, the lady's Counsel rose and said "Your Honour, my client, this lady, is the owner of a delightful piece of property, a garden spot, surrounded by shrubbery, which she agreed to rent to the defendant for a special length of time for fifty pounds. The defendant took possession, used it repeatedly for the purpose for which he had rented it, but upon leaving the premises he paid only one half the agreed rent. The rent was not excessive since this was restricted property, and we ask for judgement for the balance."

Defendant's lawyer was amused by this, but he thought it would save his client embarrassment if he replied in the same terms. "Your Honour," he said, "my client agrees that this young lady has a very attractive piece of property, that he did rent it, and derived great pleasure from the transaction. However, my client found a well on the property, around which he placed his own stones, opened a shaft, and erected a pump, supplying all his own materials, and personally using his own labour. These improvements to the property were more than enough to offset the unpaid amount, and we submit that plaintiff was adequately compensated."

The modest maiden's lawyer replied: "My client agrees that the defendant did find a well on the property, and that he did carry out the work and make the improvements described. However, had defendant not known the well was there, he would not have rented the shrubbery in the first place. Also, on giving up the lease, defendant removed his stones, pulled up the shaft, and took the pump away with him. Moreover, your Honour, in doing so he not only dragged his equipment through the shrubbery, but he left the hole much larger than it was prior to his occupancy, making it easily accessible to small boys. I ask for Judgement for the lady."

The Judge said that in view of her actions, it was only right that the young lady should be covered, and he found accordingly.

WHAT A LOVELY DEATH!

Dear Friend – this chain letter was started by a man like yourself, to bring happiness to tired business men. It costs no money! Simply send a copy to five of your business friends who are tired. Then bundle up your wife, send her to the man whose name heads the list, and add your own name.

When your name reaches the top you will receive 16,487 women, and some of them will be smashers. Have faith! One man broke the chain, and got his own wife back.

Yours sincerely, ——————

PS: At today's date a friend of mine had received 18 women. They bury him tomorrow with a smile on his face not seen there for seven years.

THE SAILORS DICTIONARY

By: Rollicking William, the Mariner.

Engineering

Naval Cutter	– Knicker elastic
Grub Screw	– Lunchtime intercourse
Endless Belt	– Night out with a sailor
Ball Race	– Tom cat 3 yds in front of Vet
Insulated Screw	– Barmaid in gumboots
Breeze Block	– Sex in the entry
Blunderbuss	– Perambulator

Love Sex and Marriage

Mothers Day	– Nine months after Fathers Day
Brassiere	– Device for making mountains out of molehills
Divorce	– When a couple can't stomach each other
Kiss	– Application at H.Q. for a position at base

Mistress	– Between a Mister and a Mattress
Prostitute	– A busybody
Salesmanship	– Difference between rape and seduction
Twins	– Womb mates who become bosom pals
Kept Woman	– One who wears mink by day and fox by night
Perfect Secretary	– One who never misses a period
Pyjamas	– Articles placed under the pillow in case of fire
Board of Trade	– A bench in Hyde Park
Love	– A fellow feeling
Jealousy	– Another fellow feeling
Taxidermist	– A man who stuffs animals
Insomnia	– When a bridegroom can't get OFF to sleep
Pansy	– One who likes vice versa
Welsh rarebit	– A Cardiff virgin
Wife	– A device which you screw on the bed and it does all the housework
Sob Sister	– A girl who sits on your knee and bawls, and makes it hard for you
Adolescence	– The time between infancy and adultery
Dancing	– Vertical expression of horizontal intention
Lady	– A woman who never smokes or drinks, and only swears when it slips out
Music Lover	– A man who hears a lady singing in the bath and puts his EAR to the keyhole
Cad	– A man who, when his girls asks for the loan of a penny, gives her two halfpennies

GEORGE TAKES UP GOLF

My wife said to me: "George, it's about time you learned to play golf – you know, that game where you chase a little ball all over the place when you're too old to chase women."

So I went to see Jones, and asked him if he would teach me to play golf. "Sure," he said "you've got balls haven't you?" I said: "Yes, but sometimes on cold mornings they're kinda hard to find."

Bring them to the Club House tomorrow, he said, and we will tee off. What's tee off? I said. He said, it's a golf term and we have to tee off in front of the Club House. Not for me, I said, you can tee off there if you want to, but I'll tee off behind a barn somewhere. No, he said, a tee is a little thing about the size of your little finger that you carry with you. Yes, I said, I've got one of those. Well, he said you stick it in the ground and put your balls on top of it. Do you play sitting down? I asked him, I always thought you walked around. He said, you stand up when you put a ball on the tee.

Well, folks, I thought that would be stretching things a bit too far, and said so. Then he asked me if I knew how to hold my club; well, after fifty years I should have some sort of an idea, so when he said you take hold of your club in both hands I knew right then he didn't know what he was talking about.

Then he said, you swing your club over your right shoulder – no! that's not me, that's my brother you're talking about. So he said, well how do you hold your club? and I said in two fingers. He said that wasn't right, and he told me to bend over and he would put two arms round me and show me how to do it. He couldn't catch me there folks! – I didn't put four years naval service in for nothing. He said, you hit your balls with your club, and they will soar and soar, and I said I could well believe that. Then he said, and when you're on the green. . . . What's the green? I asked. That's where the hole is, surely you're not colour-blind? he asked. No? then you take your putter, and you put the ball in the hole . . . you mean the putter, I corrected. He said no, the hole isn't big enough for the ball and the putter. Well – I've seen holes big enough for a horse and wagon.

Then, he said, after making the first hole, you go on and do the next seventeen. He wasn't talking to me! After two holes I'm shot to hell. You mean, he said, you can't make 18 holes in one day? Hell no, I said, it takes me 18 days to make one hole, besides I said, how will I know when I'm in the 18th hole?

He said, you'll know, because then the flag will go up. That would be just my luck.

A MAN'S LIFE

Years	Times
20 – 30	Tri-weekly
30 – 40	Try weekly
40 – 50	Try weakly
Over 50	Beer is Best

WOMEN – AND THE FIVE CONTINENTS

At 14–18 she is like Africa, partly virgin and partly explored.

At 18–24 she is like Australia, highly developed in the built up areas.

At 24–30 she is like America, highly technical, and always seeking new methods.

At 30–35 she is like Asia, sultry, hot and mysterious.

At 35–45 she is like Europe, devastated, but still interesting in places.

(At 45–65 she is like Antarctica, everybody knows where it is, but nobody wants to go there!)

INSTRUCTIONS FOR USING THE NEW
DIAL TELEPHONES

On the telephone there is a dial with letters to indicate the Exchange required. For instance, S for south, P for pussy if using the phonetic code, and O for the operator.

If south is required, put your finger in the S hole or in the P hole for pussy, according to requirements. If the operator is wanted, put your finger in the Operator's hole and work your finger until she comes, then she will give you the required connection.

If you have fingered the P hole correctly, you will hear a purring sound, but if you have inserted your finger in the wrong hole, the R's hole for instance, you will hear a high-pitched scream. In this event, remove your finger, and put the end of your pencil in pussy. When you have finished the operator may have lost her ring.

Where satisfactory connection proves difficult, this may be due to more than one person fingering the operator's hole at the same time, or the cable engineers may have slipped a length in the operator's socket. You must then wait for service until he removes his tool.

To remedy faults

Hold your instrument tightly round the middle, and feel underneath until the operator responds. Remove your finger from either the P hole or the R's hole, grasp the flex and pull your wire until you hear a buzzing in the ears.

Foreign connections

These involve the use of small French letters or else Dutch caps.

There was a young man of Bavaria
Who peed in a clergyman's area
Said the maid to the cook,
"Cook, do come and look,
"It's longer than master's, and hairier!"

There was a young fellow of Kent
Whose wick was exceedingly bent,
To save himself trouble
He had it bent double
And instead of coming, he went!

There was a young Scottie named Dave
Who kept a dead whore in a cave
And when he was told
"You'll find her too cold!"
Said: "Think o' the siller I save!"

There was a young lady named Grace
Whose corset no longer would lace,
Her mother said: "Nelly!"
"There's more in your belly,
"Than ever went in through your face!"

There was a young lady of Rye
Who said to a gent passing by:
"I've looked in my bag
And I haven't a rag. . . ."
So he gave her his Old School Tie.

Up Spake a Brave old Pauper

It was Christmas Day in the Workhouse
The one day of the year
When paupers' hearts were full of joy,
Their bellies full of beer.

Then rose the Workhouse Master
He was a wicked sod:
"You'll do your tasks this afternoon,
"Or else you get no pud."

Up spake a brave old pauper,
His face as bold as brass:
"You can keep your Christmas pudding mate
"And stuff it up your ass!"

They seized the Workhouse Master
He fought with might and main
They cut his bloody privates off
And pulled the bloody chain

BROKEN DOWN BY AGE AND SEX

In days of old, when knights were bold,
And paper not invented,
They wiped the ass, with tufts of grass
And they were quite contented

In days of old, when knights were bold,
And women not invented
They drilled great holes in telegraph poles
And they were quite contented.

MINI-POME

'Tis God who sends the roaring winds
To blow the skirts on high
But God is just and sends the dust
To blind the bad man's eye.

NURSERY RHYME

There was a little girl
And she had a little curl
Right in the middle of her forehead
And when she was good she was very very good
And when she was bad she was marvellous!

EPITAPH

Here lie the remains of Schultz's Charlotte
Who died a highly respected harlet,
For fourteen years she kept her virginity
A very long time for this vicinity.

TRIBUTE

Mae loved for profit, not for fun
And she was scorned by everyone.
Dee loved for fun, and not for profit
And made a very good thing off it!

ANOTHER MINI-POME

If skirts get any shorter,
Said the typist, with a blush,
There'll be two more cheeks to powder
And a lot more hair to brush!

LITTLE MARY'S LITTLE MARY

Little Mary pinned her hopes
On a book by Mary Stopes
Judging by the girl's condition
It must have been an old edition.

Mary had a little lamb
Its fleece was white as snow
And everywhere that Mary went
A ram was sure to go.

Mary had a little lamb. . . .
And the midwife was treated for shock!

BLACK OUTLOOK

A Labourite rose in the House for to speak
"We support the new Vice Act, the best thing this week,
Experience teaches, if life's to be sweet,
"We must shift all these floozies away from the street.
"Life will be better, I swear I'll be bound
"If we put prostitution right under the ground!"

Then up rose a Tory, a man from the Shires
He called them all spoilsports, and twisters, and liars,
"For backing this Act now, your reason is plain—
"To pamper the miners, yet once more again."

THE RADCLIFFE CAMERA
(Oxford University Reading Room)

Whenever I work in the Radder
I wish it could truly be said
That my head was as full as my bladder
My bladder as void as my head!

GODIVA PROCESSION

Early this century there was controversy whether Coventry
Corporation were right to erect only one row of stands. . . .

It was worth more than a fiva
To watch Lady Godiva –
When the wind blew off the wig
Of Miss Nan Gigg,
She continued her ride
With stands on either side

EXPENSES ACCOUNT!

In Warwick she was Winnie, she was Margaret in Perth
In Stratford she was Maisy, the sweetest thing on earth
In Brighton she was Betty, the cutest of the bunch
But down in his expenses, she was Petrol, Oil, and Lunch!

EFFLUENCE

He was our Sewage Manager, was Mr Moses Mudge
And he never thought of anything, but activated sludge,
He never heard us laughing but he gazed with great regret at us,
For his mind was just as murky as his own discoloured detritus;
Promotion had come soon to him (hard work combined with piety)
And thus he was outstanding in the Effluent Society!

FOOTPRINTS ON THE DASHBOARD,
UPSIDE DOWN

My wife bought me a lighter
And I'm such a clever blighter
That when it stuck, it didn't mean a thing —
For I'd also had a knife, from my jealous little wife
Which screws the screw that screws the little spring.

I was sitting in my car
When I got a nasty jar
While I fiddled and I twiddled at that spring. . . .
As I poked away, I cursed, for there came a sudden burst
Of metal objects, flying with a "ping!"

My search was microscopic
And I nearly went myopic
My limbs were twisted all ways and my breath was nearly stopped,
As I stretched round nooks and crannies finding peppermints of
  grannies,
But not the little lighter parts that popped.

When I found them, it was late
She was waiting at the gate,
With black suspicion written in her frown
"I've been a fool my dear. . ." but all she did was leer
At my footprints on the dashboard upside down!"

LEAVE, COMPASSIONATE, CHILDREN, FOR THE PRODUCTION OF

In 1945 troops serving abroad were offered home leave subject to certain conditions:

In distant lands the stalwart bands of would-be fathers wait,
Certificates to join their mates, upon affairs of state.
For para (3), Appendix (b), will authorise a chap
To reproduce (for scheduled use) the species Homo Sap.

When Good Sir James takes down their names, in files, to procreate
This caveat the unborn must circumnavigate :
"All who have wives past thirtyfive, and children unbegot,
And certified that they have tried, are able, and have not,
May stake a claim. But if they have not, or succeeded,
We can't allow that here and now their services are needed.
All who apply must certify, that they can understand
What lies behind the subtle mind of Middle East Command."

The Middle East has now released a gallant group of men,
Of future Dads, like Galahads, who have the strength of ten,
And every dame must be the same, for it is infra dig
That they should dare a child to bear, uncertified by Grigg.

THOUGHTS ON A.I.D.
By A COW

Though I've just given birth to a heifer
And of pride and of milk I am full
It is sad to relate that my lacteal state
Was NOT brought about by a bull.

I have never been rogered, I swear it,
In spite of the calves I have borne
I swear by that tractor, I'm virgo intacta
I never took bull by the horn!

How dreary this farmyard and meadow
This cowshed seems gloomy and grey
For the one bit of fun in the year's dreary run
By science is taken away.

I know that the farm is a business,
In which we must all pull our weight,
And I'd pull and I'd pull, for a strongly built bull,
But this phoney business I hate.

It mustn't be thought that I'm jealous
There are things a mere cow shouldn't say,
But the Land Army tarts who handle our parts
Still get it the oldfashioned way.

THE 1951 BUDGET

Big Ben it is chiming the hour is now late
The Commons are sitting in deepest debate,
Discussing the gravest of National matters,
Concerning the conduct of tarts queers and hatters.

The Chancellor rose, and said : "Striking at vice?"
"Then the easiest way is by raising the price"
"I feel certain Hon Members will never revoke"
"A Bill I'm presenting called 'Pay as you Poke'."

"The Customs and Excise will find it a cinch"
"To collect these new duties – one shilling an inch"
[Amid shouts from the House, of 'Get out!' and 'Resign']
"And I'll pay my quota each time I have mine –."

"There's the Member for Mudsport, a cuddlesome lass"
"Who performs anytime for a bottle of Bass"
"There's the Member for Ticklam, who says in a daze"
"For a packet of Woodbines she'll take it both ways."

Clem Attlee was up, on his feet in a flash
Denouncing this tariff on crumpet for cash,
And then, in a slashing attack on the Tories –
"You've stuffed benches and wenches you randy old whorers."

The Labourites raved against privilege and wealth,
Demanding free crumpet upon National Health,
While Bevin created an odour of haddocks
By pulling the pants down off Dame Molly Maddox.

Herbert Morrison tossed all the Clerks at the table
While Bevin was stroking and pulling his cable.
And the member for Tamworth enjoyed several jerks
With Postmaster General and Minister of Works.

The member for Bannock, a big buxom wench
Was waving her tits at the Government bench
And the Member for Bilston, tho' three times a grannie
Induced Ebby Edwards to tickle her fanny.

Sir Winston came in, and with V-sign and topper
Induced Lady Astor to play with his chopper
Whilst poor Hughie Gaitskell then left the front rank
And walked round the lobbies in search of a wank.

The Closure was moved then, to end the debate
Just as Black Rod was tickling the balls of his mate
Whilst Megan Lloyd George let go a right squeaker
When having it off with the Rt Hon, the Speaker.

So voters take heed, if you have an erection
There's no need to wait for a General Election
For married or widowed, bachelor or spinster
There's plenty of Crumpet and Cock at Westminster.

TENDER LOVE

Boy meets girl, holds her hand, visions of a promised land
Tender words, cling and kiss, crafty feel, heavenly bliss
Nibbles nipples, squeezes thighs, gets a beat, feels a rise,
Flies agape, drawers well down, really starts to go to town,
Legs outspread, virgin lass, fanny froths like bottled bass.
Love is great, a Cupid stunt, soon he'll feel a stupid. . . .

Love's a jewel, pearls he's won, shoots his load — what's he done?
Comes the pay-off, here's the rub, now she's in the Pudding Club!
Shotgun wedding, bridesmaids flap, Love and Cherish, all that crap.
A tubby tummy, weight she gains, prams and nappies, labour pains,
Realises what he did, nagging missus, shrieking kid.

Sweats his balls off, works his stint, all the same he's always skint,
Only pleasure, evenings when, mattress creaks she's off again.
Can't forsake those sexy habits, breeding kids like bleeding rabbits,
Curses marriage, starts to bicker, swears he'll choke the bleeding vicar.
Work and worry take their toll, gets cheesed off with same old hole.

Bit of fluff, quite a kick, auburn hair, likes her dick,
Gets it in, lovely fit, durex bursts, he's in the shit.
Up in Court, nowt to say, ten at home, one away,
That silky hole with hair all round has dug his grave in stony ground.
As he draws his final breath, knows he's shagged himself to death,
On his tombstone, plainly lacquered, his epitaph, just
    f***ing knackered!

There was a young lady named Joan
Who went to the dentist's alone
In a fit of depravity
He filled the wrong cavity
She nurses the filling at home.

There was a young fellow named Hyde
Who fell down a closet and died;
He had a brother
Who fell down another,
And now they're interred side by side.

There was a young man of Cawnpore
Whose dick was one inch and no more,
It was lovely for keyholes
And little girls' peeholes
But lost in a bloody great whore!

There was a young lady of Exeter
And all the young men craned their necks at 'er,
Save one dirty sod
Who did six months in quod
Far waving his organ of sex at 'er.

There was a young lady of Gloucester
Whose parents thought they had lost her,
But they found in the grass
The marks of her ass,
And the knees of the man who had crossed her!

Warner now offers an exciting range of quality titles by both established and new authors. All of the books in this series are available from:
Little, Brown and Company (UK),
P.O. Box 11,
Falmouth,
Cornwall TR10 9EN.

Alternatively you may fax your order to the above address. Fax No. 0326 376423.

Payments can be made as follows: Cheque, postal order (payable to Little, Brown and Company) or by credit cards, Visa/Access. Do not send cash or currency. UK customers: and B.F.P.O.: please send a cheque or postal order (no currency) and allow £1.00 for postage and packing for the first book, plus 50p for the second book, plus 30p for each additional book up to a maximum charge of £3.00 (7 books plus).

Overseas customers including Ireland, please allow £2.00 for postage and packing for the first book, plus £1.00 for the second book, plus 50p for each additional book.

NAME (Block Letters) ....

ADDRESS...

....

☐ I enclose my remittance for _____

☐ I wish to pay by Access/Visa Card

Number ☐☐☐☐☐☐☐☐☐☐☐☐☐☐☐☐

Card Expiry Date ☐☐☐☐